Some of the BIG IDEAS that will challenge

How to experience **The Phenomenon**— next 12 months than in the previous 12 years.

Do you suffer from **Wealth Inhibition?**

You do **not** get what you deserve.

The **difference** between the wealthy entrepreneurs and the also-rans is *not* as great as most believe.

Positive Thinking alone is **worthless.**

What is your **#1** Entrepreneurial Responsibility?

Is there a **"dirty little secret"** behind many wealthy entrepreneurs?

The **worst** of all wealth-defeating habits is . . .

YCDBSOYA

Are you an "opportunity thinker"—or are you **guilty** of "outcome thinking"?

"Do what you love and the money will follow" is **B.S.** hazardous to your wealth.

Stop playing **Blind Archery**

12 Ways to Increase Your **"Personal** Value"

Why you must **STOP thinking about Income!**

You need your own **Zero Tolerance Policy** about . . .

The 90-Day Experiment that may change your life forever.

"I am now implementing some of your techniques and wanted to let you know that the best piece of advice you gave me was . . ." (Note: it's in this book, in Wealth Magnet 14.) "As of today, I have already gotten **over $60,000.00 (in one week)** . . . I again want to thank you. I am grateful for your No B.S. approach."

—David C. Gross, New York, 144 Music And Arts Inc., www.144musicandarts.com
David's company is a leader in the new, expanding field of outsourced teaching artists, providing professional musicians and artists as well as equipment to public schools on contract.

"Last week I celebrated my 50th birthday. After the party, I thought about how much I have to be thankful for. I thought of you immediately. I now have **more money than I'll probably need for the rest of my life.** So much of the credit for that goes to you. Yeah, I know money isn't everything. But money buys you freedom, and freedom is everything. Thank you so much."

—Paul Hartunian, New Jersey, www.paulhartunian.com
Paul is the leading authority on do-it-yourself publicity. He helps thousands of entrepreneurs obtain local and national print and broadcast media exposure, and has himself been on dozens of major talk shows, including *The Tonight Show*, and hundreds of radio programs, featured in *Forbes*, etc. He is "the man who sold the Brooklyn Bridge."

"You've helped us make money since 1993, and many of your ideas have earned us a small fortune."

—T. J. Rohleder, M.O.R.E. Inc., Kansas
T.J. is the owner of a giant publishing/mail-order business generating millions of dollars annually. He started from scratch, with one simple idea and one advertisement.

"The specific advice you give is obviously valuable, but what has been even more important is your way of thinking and how I have been led to **see much greater opportunities."**

—Jerry Jones, Oregon
Jerry has a Bonus Chapter in this book.

"If I haven't said 'thanks' lately, I'm overdue. You've been an awesome help to me in my business and in my personal life, in my outlook. **I've got a couple of really nice houses and cars thanks to you, too!"**

—Ron Caruthers, California
Ron has a Bonus Chapter in this book.

"My friend Dan Kennedy is unique, a genius in many ways. I have always admired his ability to **see the vital truths in any business and to state these realities with straight language and clear definitions.** His approach is direct. His ideas are controversial. His ability to get results for his clients unchallenged. What you discover in the pages ahead will **change your business life and income forever."**

—Brian Tracy. www.briantracy.com
Brian is one of America's most sought after and popular professional speakers and the author of dozens of outstanding business books, including *Turbo Strategy: 21 Ways To transform Your Business*. This comment is from Brian's introduction to another book In the No B.S. serles, *No B.S. Business Success*.

"After 8 or 9 years' association with Dan, I'm still learning.....his ideas have **created millions and millions of dollars** of revenue for us."
—Ron LeGrand, www.globalpublishinginc.com

Ron is the author of *Quick Turn Real Estate*, and is the number-one authority and "grand-daddy" of the entire industry of independent real estate entrepreneurs who buy and flip properties for big, fast profits. Virtually every other expert in this field has been a Ron LeGrand student. Ron has personally done thousands of real estate transactions, and combined with his students—many of whom have become millionaires in short time—turns over hundreds of millions of dollars of real estate every year.

For a larger collection of client and student comments about Dan Kennedy's work as well as information about his other books, newsletters, and services, visit these web sites:

www.nobsbooks.com
www.dankennedy.com
www.dankennedywebstore.com
www.nationalsaleslettercontest.com

N○B.S.
WEALTH ATTRACTION
FOR ENTREPRENEURS

THE ULTIMATE
NO HOLDS BARRED
KICK BUTT
TAKE NO PRISONERS
GUIDE TO REALLY
GETTING RICH

Dan Kennedy

EP
Entrepreneur.
Press

Editorial Director: Jere L. Calmes
Cover Design: David Shaw
Production and Composition: Eliot House Productions

This publication is designed to provide accurate and authoritative information in regard to the subject matter covered. It is sold with the understanding that the publisher is not engaged in rendering legal, accounting or
other professional services. If legal advice or other expert assistance is
required, the services of a competent professional person should be sought.

Library of Congress Cataloging-in-Publication Data
Kennedy, Dan S., 1954–
    No B.S. guide to wealth attraction for entrepreneurs: the ultimate, no
holds barred, kick butt, take no prisoners guide to really getting
rich/by Dan S. Kennedy.
       p.   cm.
    ISBN 13 : 978-193253167-1 (alk. paper)
    ISBN 10 : 1-932531-67-X (alk. paper)
    1. Success in business. 2. Entrepreneurship. 3. Business enterprises. I.
Title: No BS guide to wealth attraction for entrepreneurs. II. Title.
HF5386.K27654 2006
658.15'224—dc22   2005027239

Printed in Canada
12 11 10 09 08   10 9 8 7 6 5

Contents

Acknowledgments

This book owes an enormous debt, as do I, to Andrew Carnegie, Napoleon Hill, W. Clement Stone, Dr. Edward L. Kramer, Sidney Newton Bremer, and my personal friend and associate, Foster Hibbard.

Preface

How to Make Yourself Magnetic to Money

This not a book about MAKING money.

This is not a book about CREATING wealth. Both words, "making" and "creating," reinforce what I call The Work-Money Link, a limiting idea that I will change, a chain I will break in this book. Words like "MAKE" or "CREATE" suggest that you obtain wealth through and in proportion to the effort exerted. These words imply that wealth comes about primarily, if not only, through hard work, through extreme exertion.

This book is about the *attraction* of wealth.

I use the word "attraction" most deliberately.

In this book, I hope to empower and equip you to attract all the wealth you want. With far greater ease than you've ever imagined. Faster than you think possible. With less work than you would think possible.

This is a radical shift on several levels.

There is a philosophical component, so I will be discussing your thoughts and attitudes and beliefs about wealth. But I will not stop there. As an early mentor of mine said, you can't eat philosophy. There is a way of thinking that repels wealth, and obviously that is how most people think. There is a way to think that attracts wealth. If you think that way, you are magnetic to opportunity, money, and wealth.

There is a strategic component. There are very practical things to do to put yourself in the right position, to set in motion the forces that attract wealth. I'm not talking about investing strategies; this is not a book about investing, although there are Bonus Chapters from some of my own hand-picked, expert advisors on very specific investment, money management, and opportunity strategies. You invest to create or preserve wealth. I'm talking about the attraction of wealth. So relax, you need not fear yet another mind-numbing discussion of mutual funds, 401Ks, and stocks and trends illustrated with charts and graphs. Instead, I'll be dealing with entrepreneurial strategies, relationship strategies, influence strategies, and marketing strategies that, properly employed, make you magnetic to opportunity, money, and wealth.

Finally, there is a behavioral component. There are behaviors that repel wealth, and that is, obviously, how most people behave. There are ways to behave that attract wealth. If you behave that way, you are magnetic to opportunity, money, and wealth.

In total, this is all about making adjustments to the way you think and act that make it easier to attract all the wealth you want, faster and easier than you can imagine.

WARNING!

Yes, a warning. When I say radical changes in beliefs and behavior, I mean it. A lot of what you are about to read is going to be very hard to swallow. You will be tempted to reject it instantly. You will find it contrary and challenging to what you've been taught and what you believe. It will make you uncomfortable. It's natural to simply turn off and move away from anything causing you discomfort. However, a great deal of discovery, growth, progress, and success is preceded by discomfort.

This is a _very_ blunt book. Its No B.S. title makes that promise. And a lot of what is published elsewhere about wealth is in the feel-good category. This book includes a fair amount of things those other authors probably know but keep to themselves, lacking the courage to say them publicly, certain they will offend people. I have never been concerned about who I may offend and I'm not about to start worrying about it now. I didn't even sugarcoat many of these discomfort producing statements, building up to them gently, wrapping them in entertaining parables. So as Katherine Hepburn said, get ready for a bumpy ride! This IS the No B.S. truth about how entrepreneurs attract wealth as I know it.

To avoid having wasted the price of this book, and more importantly, to avoid missing out on incredible opportunities to transform your life for the better, you need to tolerate some of this discomfort, to patiently and carefully consider ideas and suggestions that at first seem dead wrong, illogical, irrational, and unreasonable to you.

To encourage you, I'm going to briefly describe my "qualifications," to convince you that I am a person you should take seriously, even though I'm presenting ideas you find difficult to accept. I tell you these things not to brag. I have no need.

I started out in life broke, with no family resources. I have no college degree. By traditional measurements and predictive factors, I'm a man least likely to succeed. Before age 50, solely via my own entrepreneurial pursuits, I had amassed sufficient wealth to allow me to stop working and never make another dollar if I so chose. I have built, bought, and sold businesses, developed hugely successful businesses, and even invented an entire industry. I have achieved prominence, and some degree of fame. In recent years, money has flowed to me in ever-increasing abundance even as my interest in it has waned. I have made millions of dollars a year in personal income. I own a nice home, own many racehorses, have zero debt, and live exactly as I wish in every respect. I work closely, privately with hundreds of multi-millionaire and seven-figure-income entrepreneurs, most of whom have created their businesses from scratch—many quickly and many with my assistance from the start. These millionaires literally stand in line and pay huge sums for my advice. These people take me very seriously. I have taught them how to go beyond the making of money to the easy attraction of wealth.

This book, incidentally, is derived in part from a seminar I conducted only once (by my choice), attended by about 100 entrepreneurs, each paying about $1,000.00 for the privilege. It is also based in part on discussions from a Wealth Attraction Coaching Group that I worked with. It was comprised of 18 entrepreneurs, most enjoying million- and multimillion-dollar annual incomes, each paying $14,000.00 to be in the group. My lowest consulting fee is currently $9,200.00 for a day, a substantially higher hourly rate than top lawyers and law firms or top doctors can command.

Again, I tell you all this to evidence the value and validity of the ideas in this book, even though they may seem weird to you.

If you stop to think about it, it's probably true that most of what you've been taught about money, opportunity, and wealth was taught to you by people without wealth. Most of what you've read or heard about wealth was said or written by the unwealthy. Most of the people you've associated with, whose opinions about money you've heard often, aren't wealthy. Most of what is your present belief system about wealth was built with raw material you obtained from unwealthy sources.

In stark contrast to those sources, I am a wealthy source. If my ideas didn't contradict, conflict, and challenge those in your present belief system, something would be wrong!

Incidentally, I fully realize you may be quite successful in your own right. I suspect that's the case. Poor people rarely buy books with "wealth" in the title, just one of the many reasons they stay poor. So I do not discount your accomplishments or your knowledge. But I've worked with a great many successful people who struggled mightily to get there, who succeed in spite of their beliefs about wealth rather than thanks to them. I have watched such people go through the most amazing transformations and liberation with the ideas in this book. I will tell you about some of them in the book. No matter how successful you may be, I am confident you will find some ideas in this book that will surprise you, shock you, challenge you, liberate you, and benefit you. I am confident that Donald Trump could read this book and find something to use, to attract even greater wealth, easier than ever before.

How to Get a Collection of Wealth Attraction Tools—Free

I am eager for the ideas in this book to work for you, for you to put them to work for you. For that reason, I have assembled an entire Wealth Attraction Tool Kit, which includes an Action Guide for this book, checklists, forms, Psychological Trigger Cards, a teleseminar, and an e-mail course. To get your collection, you need to go online to www.nobsbooks.com, to the section linked to this book.

Book Roadmap

Section I has 26 Wealth Magnets. I have kept the explanation of each as brief as possible. They are not in a sequential order, like steps 1, 2, and 3. Instead, you might think of these as more like puzzle pieces laid out on a table, waiting for you to fit them together in a way that works best for you. You can also treat this section as a cafeteria line, choosing whatever Magnets seem most important to you at the moment. As you will see, some are philosophical, some very practical. The entrepreneur needs both: a personal philosophy about wealth, a view of the way wealth moves in the world, and a set of practical strategies, tools, and skills.

Section II is a collection of Bonus Chapters from experts on different aspects of investment, financial opportunities, and wealth management. Each chapter is from a different authority.

These are people I work with closely in different ways, whom I invited to contribute. These chapters were prepared exclusively for this book.

Section III, Wealth Resources, includes a directory of contact information for the experts contributing articles, many of the other people mentioned throughout the book, and people you need to meet and books you must read if you are very serious about wealth. Free Offers and Resources start on page 294. These include two tickets to a $995.00 per person seminar—free and a three-month Gold Inner Circle Membership, which includes my *No B.S. Marketing Letter* free.

The audio CD included contains selected excerpts from recordings of my Wealth Attraction Seminar, my Renegade Millionaire System, and other programs. An online catalog of all my programs is at www.dankennedywebstore.com.

"Our brains become magnetized
with the dominating thoughts
which we hold in our minds, and,
by means with which no man is familiar,
these 'magnets' attract to us
the forces, the people,
the circumstances of life
which harmonize with the nature of
our dominating thoughts."

—NAPOLEON HILL,

AUTHOR OF LAWS OF SUCCESS,

THINK AND GROW RICH,

GROW RICH WITH PEACE OF MIND

WWW.NAPOLEONHILL.COM

SECTION I

WEALTH MAGNETS

Wealth Magnet 1
No Guilt

Most peoples' world view of wealth is as a zero sum game. A big impediment to attraction of wealth is the idea that the amount of wealth floating around to be attracted is limited. If you believe it's limited, then you believe that each dollar you get came to you at someone else's expense; your gain another's loss. That makes your subconscious mind queasy. So it keeps your wealth attraction power turned down, never on full power. To let it operate on full power would be unfair and harmful to others. If you are a decent human being, and you have this viewpoint, then you will always modulate your wealth attraction power. If too much starts pouring in too easily, guilt is produced as if it were insulin being produced by the pancreas after pigging out on a whole pizza. You can't help it. Your wealth magnetism will be turned down *for you*.

Think about the words "fair share."

They are powerful, dangerous words.

As an ethical, moral person, you probably think—*Hey, I don't want more than my fair share.* But that reveals belief that wealth is limited. If you believe wealth is unlimited, there's no such thing as a share of it. Everybody's share is unlimited. There's nothing to have a share of. There's only unlimited. Your fair share is all you can possibly attract, as is anybody and everybody else's.

In business, there's a similar idea: market share. But again that presumes a finite, limited market, instead of an infinitely expandable market.

A Tale of Two Teenagers

Imagine being a teenager in a family in severe financial trouble. Money is very scarce. There's you, two brothers, father, and mother. When everybody sits down to dinner and Mom puts the food on the table, you know that's all the food there is. The bowl of mashed potatoes is all the mashed potatoes there are. You are hungry. You really want a big second helping of mashed potatoes. The bowl is right in front of you within easy reach. But instead of just reaching out, dragging it over, and scooping out a pile of potatoes, you stop to look around to see who has potatoes on their plates. You look to see if your father's had plenty of potatoes. You hold back from fulfilling your desire out of concern that others may not yet have had their fair share, that someone may be hungrier than you. You do not want someone else going hungry as result of your appetite.

I don't have to imagine that. I lived it.

Now imagine being a teenager in a family living an abundant life with great prosperity. When Mom puts dinner on the table, you know there's plenty more where it came from. The refrigerator's full of food. So are the cupboards. There are always leftovers after dinner. You are hungry. You really want a big second helping of mashed potatoes. The bowl is right in front of you within easy reach. Without a second thought, you'll reach out, drag the bowl over, and scoop out all the potatoes you want.

In these examples, of course, you're acting consciously. In the first case, in the financially troubled family, you consciously hold back, sacrifice, do not take what is right in front of you for the taking.

Similarly but subconsciously, if you believe at all on any level that wealth is limited, that there's *not* plenty to go around, you will hold back; you won't take everything that's right in front of you. Your emotions about wealth will be cautious, measured, restricted, suppressed, and timid.

If you can make every last smidgen of belief that wealth is limited go away, your attraction of wealth will suddenly, automatically go from modulated, limited, and suppressed to full power, and opportunity, money, and wealth will quickly flow to you in greater quantities at greater speed than you've ever before experienced.

People actually think and get ingrained in their heads that money taken from Person A and moved to Person B enriches Person B at the expense of Person A. Certainly, the liberal politicians either believe it or pander to it, one way or the other. Some religious doctrines and religious leaders posit this idea. There are lots of ways you might get this belief firmly planted in your head, maybe even in elementary school math class. If Johnny has four pieces of candy and gives two of them to Jim, how many does Johnny have left? The answer needed to ace the quiz is two. But the math problem ignores the fact that Johnny can simply open his hand and have as many pieces of candy appear in it as he'd like. After all, there's no global shortage of candy. When you actually understand wealth, you know that Johnny can have 4 pieces, give Jim 2 pieces, but then have 42 pieces.

What's even weirder and tougher for math teachers is that Johnny is much more likely to have 42 if he does give away 2 of the 4 than if he hoards the 4. But that's another topic for a different place in this book. For now, let's keep it simple:

> The opposite of wealth
> attraction is wealth inhibition.

Most people never even think in terms of getting wealthy. Their thoughts on this subject are limited to buying a lottery ticket or fantasizing about some unknown, long-lost uncle leaving them a fortune in his will. But there are a lot of people who do, at some point, start seriously trying to figure out how they might convert their knowledge, ability, time, energy, and effort into real wealth. You may be in that group—it may be the reason you were attracted to and purchased this book. So, a warning: the majority of people in this group never get traction, never get going, never get wealthy because they suffer from wealth inhibition.

If you believe wealth is limited, if you view it as a zero sum game, you are inhibited. This inhibition affects all sorts of things you do or don't do, such as what you'll charge or who you'll ask for money.

I've spent a lot of time working with people in sales and with those who identify themselves as salespeople, like folks selling insurance, cars, and fire alarms, as well as those who don't identify themselves as salespeople but are, like dentists and psychologists. Two things that reflect wealth inhibition are true for all of them.

One has to do with price. Most fear discussion of price, fear raising prices, and are paranoid about pricing higher than their competitors. I have had to work long and hard to get some people to raise their prices or fees far beyond present levels, industry norms, or competitors' in order to charge what their service and expertise are really worth to their clientele. In numerous cases, I've forced fee or price increases of 200% to 2,000% with absolutely no adverse impact—that's how far underpriced a lot of people are! In these situations, I am not dealing with practical issues; I am dealing with the businessperson's own inhibitions and fears.

Second is pulling the punch when closing the sale. I sometimes joke about one of my own businesses, freelance advertising copywriting, where I routinely charge fees of $30,000.00 to $70,000.00 or more for a complete project and no less than $15,000.00 for a single ad or sales letter, plus royalties. I say that the primary requirement for getting such fees has nothing to do with my prowess as a copywriter and everything to do with my ability to keep a straight face and a voice free of stammer when quoting the fee! This may be the reason a lot of art and antique dealers write the price down on a piece of stationery and slide it across the desk to you. There's truth in the joke. When the dentist quotes his $70,000.00 case to the patient, when the private residence club quotes the $215,000.00 membership fee, when anyone speaks any price or fee, there is the tendency for tremors. The temptation is to discount without ever even being asked, out of fear, inhibition, and presumption—in short, to pull the punch.

Consider the salesman who goes into a person's home to sell fire alarms. (I have a corporate client in this industry.) The fire alarm salesman with the stuffed Dalmatian under his arm and the burning house video marches into the house and discovers that he is in a place of relative poverty, at least by his standards. The two kids are on a thread-bare carpet in the living room. They probably have a good television, but pretty much everything else in the house is obviously hand-me-down, beat-up, falling apart, springs sticking up out of the couch seat. He can clearly see that these people aren't doing well. Conversationally, he discovers papa hasn't worked in four months and the kid's got some kind of problem that causes big medical bills, and on and on and on. The salesperson becomes increasingly queasy about closing these people on the $1,000.00 fire alarm sale. And in many cases, he will not close the sale. He will subconsciously pull his punches, accept the first objection easily. Or he'll consciously, deliberately throw the game at the end, toss that one aside, and get out of there.

This is an analogy to the way everybody behaves in all sorts of situations if operating from a belief of limited wealth.

My friend Glenn Turner tells a story from his earliest selling days of actually being chased by somebody who was mad that he wouldn't sell him a sewing machine. Glenn thought the person couldn't afford it, shouldn't go in debt to buy it, and obviously cut his presentation short and abruptly got up and left. He was literally chased down the street and caught by the husband, who called him on not trying to make the sale, "How dare you think for me? I've got a right to buy that thing for my wife if I want to."

My speaking colleague Zig Ziglar has a similar story from his earliest days selling cookware, about the customer that was saving up the money to put in indoor plumbing. Discovering that they didn't even have indoor plumbing, Zig backed off and didn't try to close the sale on the cookware. The people were annoyed, and they really wanted the pots and pans. The husband said, "We can put the plumbing in later. Mamma wants those pots now."

The queasiness about price, about who somebody is selling to, about their ability to pay, and about their ability to afford it is all deadly. And the truth is, anytime you start to make those decisions for other people, it really reflects more about what's going on internally with you than it does about anything else.

There's something else to get clear about. People who are without money, who you perceive to be disadvantaged for one reason or another, and whom you question whether you should sell to are going to be without money next week, too, regardless of whether you get any of their money.

The reason they're without money has absolutely nothing whatsoever to do with your existence, what you sell or fail to sell, nor does it have to do with the way money works in the real world. It has to do with them. And whether you take it, somebody else takes it, the liquor store takes it, the church takes it, or who-ever takes it, I promise you somebody's getting it. Because if they're without money now, they're going to be without money again. And most of them are going to be without money perma-nently because they never gain or act on an understanding of how money works.

I know that sounds harsh. And you may not be a face-to-face salesperson and never need to sit across a desk or table from someone you think can't afford it and sell to him anyway. But the truth about this particular situation is the bigger truth about the entire world of money and wealth. That truth is, whatever amount you get has nothing to do with how much or how little anyone else has. Ever.

If you want your wealth attraction glowing and functioning at full power, you can't have *any* queasiness. You can't have *any* reluctance. You can't have *any* inhibition. You can't ever pull a punch. In the bigger sense, you have to understand that whatever financial position anyone you know is in, anyone you do busi-ness with is in, or anyone period, is in has nothing to do with you. In the biggest sense, you have to understand that whatever the state of economic affairs in the world, it has nothing to do with how much wealth you accumulate. *Your wealth is addition for you but subtraction for no one.*

Unless and until you buy this premise hook, line, and sinker, you will always suffer from wealth inhibition.

"Be clear, be truthful.
Stand there proudly,
unapologetically,
unabashedly, and say,
'I love cash.
It will get me
everything
I want in life.' "

—GENE SIMMONS, KISS
AUTHOR, *SEX, MONEY, KISS*

Wealth Magnet 2
Unequivocal Belief in Abundance

Water, water everywhere but not a drop to drink. Well, our world is no desert island. There's money, money every-where. Drink all you want.

If you do not hang out with people who own private planes, have shares in private jets, or at least fly first class everywhere they go . . . . If you do not hang out with people who have their shirts and suits custom tailored . . . . If you do not hang out with people who own racehorses or boats or vacation homes . . . . If you do not hang out with people who are extremely prosperous and adept at wealth attraction, you might be fooled into thinking that money is "tight," in limited supply or hard to come by, and based on those thoughts, you might inhibit your own wealth attraction. Or you might think such people are rare, in small number. They are not. In fact, what demographers and marketers call the "mass affluent" represent the fastest growing segment of the population. The rising tide of affluency is so great I even added a newsletter to my stable, which I edit, devoted entirely to marketing to the affluent.*

*For information about the special newsletter devoted exclusively to marketing to the affluent as well as my *No B.S. Marketing Letter*, visit www.dankennedy.com. Also, a detailed chapter about marketing to the affluent appears in another book in the No B.S. series, *No B.S. Direct Marketing for NON-Direct Marketing Businesses*.

I suggest the following experiences: visit the Forum Shops in Las Vegas, Rodeo Drive in Beverly Hills, and Bergdorf Goodman in New York City. Vacation in Boca Raton, Florida; Scottsdale, Arizona; and Aspen, Colorado. Immediately go to your nearest bookstore and pick up copies of *The Robb Report, Millionaire, Worth,* and *Town & Country* magazines. Go on a field trip to a classic car auction or a racehorse auction. In short, in person and at a distance through media, immerse yourself in the lifestyles of the affluent. Not only will you be surprised at the prices cheerfully paid for goods and services, you'll be more amazed at the vast array of very high-priced goods and services designed for affluent consumers. And, you'll be even more amazed at just how many affluent consumers there are.

The more aware you make your own mind—conscious and subconscious—of just how much affluence there is, just how much money is moving around, the more easily you will attract wealth. This is no idle exercise I suggest. It is an important step in conditioning your mind to attract wealth. Just as your body must be conditioned for health and fitness and longevity, your mind must be conditioned for wealth. Observing money flowing from the affluent is such an important and beneficial exercise, I have taken one of my Wealth Attraction Coaching Groups to Disney's Animal Kingdom Lodge on a "field trip," all staying on the concierge floor, taking the Sunrise Safari, lunching with a staff Imagineer, and eating in the five-star restaurants. I took my Gold/VIP Coaching Groups on a field trip to the Forum Shops. I give subscriptions to *The Robb Report* as client gifts. Even if you are not yet living an affluent lifestyle, you must immerse yourself in expanded awareness of what it is like and how many people are already living it.

To believe the streets are awash with money, you need to see streets awash with money. If there aren't any in your own neighborhood, you just need to get out more!

One of the past year's holiday season catalogs called *Gentleman's Domain* featured a product from the Eli Bridge Company, a manufacturer that builds amusement park rides. They've been building them for the amusement park industry for 100 years. Now, for a mere $300,000.00, they'll put the real thing in your backyard. They'll build you a 67-foot-high, 16-seat Ferris wheel. You'll need a 220 volt power outlet. And because it weighs almost 20 tons, you may want to have the patio checked out before getting started.

Of course, most peoples' reaction to an outrageous example like this is to cry "irrelevant." After all, your customers don't have this kind of money to blow; your customers are tight-fisted cheapskates; you have a hard time selling to your customers, yada yada. Pfui. A few years back, I produced an infomercial-style video brochure for a client of mine, The Shed Shop, in northern California. This company builds top-of-the-line, expensive backyard sheds. Not the tin jobs you think of. These are more like miniature houses, with peaked roofs, doors, windows, and flower boxes, and with complete interiors, with workbenches, bookshelves, and cabinetry. To shoot the video, I took a crew to a number of the customers' backyards to see their sheds and tape their testimonial comments.

One happy couple with not one but two sheds in their backyard, his and hers, are both retired. They're on Social Security, and he's got one small pension. They're totally on a fixed income. *Two* sheds.

Another guy with the biggest shed and a big pond in his backyard started out telling me something of a sob story. If you heard that, you'd assume he didn't have two nickels to rub together. But somehow, miraculously, he dug up about $20,000.00 for landscaping and a koi pond, and another $10,000.00 for the shed.

The truth all smart marketers know is: everybody somehow has plenty of money to buy whatever they decide they want to buy.

Lots of people complain about how tough they have it raising a family, having three kids, both parents having to work.

Both parents and all three kids have cellphones, which is about $90.00 a month in charges. Both of the older kids are in not one but several activities: dance, karate, Little League. Both parents drive big, new, gas-guzzling SUVs. There's a satellite dish on the side of the house, a big screen TV in the den, and a TV in every bedroom. They wouldn't know "tough" if it bit 'em in the butt, and they freely buy whatever they decide to buy.

It is a huge, huge, huge mistake for you to accept any part of the suggestion that money's tight or hard to get, that your customers don't have money or won't spend it. And if by some freak, rare, incredible chance you actually have managed to put yourself into a position where the people you are doing business with are short of money or are tight about spending it, bubba, you choose your customers. Switch to those who freely spend. There are plenty of them out there. The trend is toward mass affluence. Get with it.

Beware the news media. For some perverse reasons of its own, about which I have my suspicions, the mainstream media constantly underreports good economic news and overhypes bad economic news. During one of the weeks I was working on this book, the following news items could be found buried on page 48 of the newspaper but was quickly mentioned on CNN: New unemployment claims for preceding month were a full 1% less than projected and reduced from the prior month; the federal deficit was reduced by $133 billion; corporate taxes paid were up 40% over the prior year. That Friday, *USA Today* ran an editorial grudgingly citing these facts but interpreting it as an improvement from "depressing to dismal." The news program I watched on TV covered them all in under 2 minutes and then devoted 12 minutes to a story on high gasoline prices and a panel of supposed experts speculating on doom scenarios if gas prices continue to rise. It is a huge, huge, huge mistake for you to accept the mainstream media's biased, liberal-agenda-driven misrepresentation of the state of the economy or of the amount and level of opportunity in this country. And whatever you do, do NOT listen to any of the even more outrageously inaccurate assertions from Michael Moore and his ilk. There is a contingent of Moore-types who insist on promoting the idea that there is a teeny, tiny group of evil rich versus a gigantic population of viciously oppressed masses for whom there is no opportunity. The spew of Moore and others who echo it is toxic. I have written a lengthy article about this, originally intended for the *No B.S. Business Success* book, omitted through editorial decisions, and subsequently published in my autobiography, which you can find information about at www.renegademillionaire.com.

The truth is that the biggest, fastest growing, most expansive, and expanding segment of the American population is the mass affluent, not the poor.

Here's something interesting about affluence. I was born in 1954. Owning the color TV in the neighborhood was a sign of affluence. When I was a kid, we were the only people in our entire neighborhood near Cleveland, Ohio, to have a swimming pool. That was a big deal. Getting a new car, a big deal. In the '70s, the two-car household was affluent. Now it's a two-house household. Not long ago, on a flight from Cleveland to Orlando, I realized through conversation that every single person in the first class seats owned a home in Cleveland and another home in Florida. There is, right now, this minute, more disposable income by any measurement—dollars, percentages, ratios, you pick the statistics you like—than ever before. There are more people invested in real estate in addition to their homes and in the stock market than ever. There are more millionaires than ever before. There will be the biggest wealth transfer in American history from my generation to the next.

On top of that, new categories of products and services, new entertainments and recreations, new industries, new opportunities abound. Stop and think about all the businesses that didn't even exist when you were a kid. I marvel at it all.

I am also absolutely convinced that if you don't do well financially in America today, it is either due to utter ignorance of opportunity or choice. It definitely is NOT due to lack of opportunity.

These fact-based beliefs are essential to turning off wealth inhibition and turning up wealth attraction. If you do not share these beliefs, if you doubt and question the fact of unlimited, readily available abundance of both opportunity and money, then you need to invest time and energy on your own fact-finding research mission and make this sale to yourself. Otherwise, to borrow from a friend, the late Jim Newman, author of the fine book *Release Your Brakes,* you are driving down the highway to wealth with one foot on the gas but the other riding the brake.

Wealth Magnet 3
Break Free of "Fairness"

A lot of the authors, speakers, and teachers of "prosperity" in the metaphysical community are far from prosperous themselves. Over the years, quite a few have privately confessed their lack of financial success to me and expressed puzzlement over it. Typically, the conversation has to do with their idea of "justice." They believe because they do "good work" that they deserve to be wealthy and that wealth should occur. There are also a lot of these people who perpetually beat themselves up with the idea that their lack of financial success is about their somehow not deserving it, so they need to work on themselves in order to be more deserving persons.

One of the leading companies teaching negotiation skills to corporate executives, Charles Karrass' company, has this as its slogan:

You don't get what you deserve. You get what you negotiate.

The metaphysical version of this is, "I'm just not using the mental principles well enough. If I just think more positively (key word "just"), things will turn around."

If you compare the two ideas, you'll see that the metaphysical version puts the responsibility for what will happen "out there." *Things* will turn around. Not that *you* will turn things around. It's a difference between passive and active. The statement about negotiation puts the responsibility for outcomes on you. And it acknowledges a very important fact: the marketplace does not function on fairness. If that were true, top talent would always win out. The made-by-*American-Idol* William Huang would never have had a hit record.

To rewrite the Karrass statement, I would say, "You don't get what you (inherently) deserve. You get what you deliberately and intentionally attract, by who you are but also by what you think, say and do, and get others to do."

Being a moral, spiritual, "good," deserving person alone is just not sufficient. In a purely fair marketplace, it might be. But it isn't.

An extension of this sort of thinking is the surprisingly popular argument that 9/11 was the United States' fault, in whole or part, because it has so much and other countries have so little, and because it has an immoral society. So if Americans were just more moral and more generous, they wouldn't deserve what happened on 9/11, and it never would have happened. Therefore, the United States should close the Defense Department, take all that money and divide it up among the less-fortunate people in all these other countries, and spend it on churches and moral education in this country. Americans don't need a Defense Department. If they are just "better people," they'll be more deserving of peace and tranquility and security, and they'll have it. This idea is championed by fools. If you want to philosophically fantasize that this is the way the world should work, that's fine. But don't suggest it's the way the world does work.

Money has no moral conscience. It finds its way into the hands of pornographers just as it does into the hands of Bible publishers. And I mean no disrespect to either. Trying to impose your opinions of "good" and "bad," "moral" and "immoral," "deserving" and "undeserving" onto money is even more futile than trying to impose them on people. This is a very difficult principle of wealth attraction to accept, but I urge you try.

> "Rules such as 'if I hold positive thoughts about prosperity, money will just start pouring into my life' are just too simplistic to work . . . money exists in the physical domain. Money doesn't come as the result of thoughts in the metaphysical realm; it comes as the result of actions in the physical domain."
>
> —MARIA NEMETH, PH.D.
> *THE ENERGY OF MONEY*

Money moves based on nonjudgmental market forces, not morality. The difficult truth is that being a good person, being a better person, does not automatically entitle you to wealth, nor does it do anything to directly strengthen your wealth attraction. If you think that you should be financially rewarded because you are honest, hard-working, and kind to old people and pets, you're in for a very disappointing life. If you think God should intervene with the lotto on your behalf because you volunteer at the soup kitchen, you'll wind up disliking God.

If you want to easily attract a lot of money, you have to come to grips with what money is and isn't, the very nature of money, the energy of money, and how money moves about from one home to another.

Money doesn't have a conscience. It's paper. That's all it is. It's just paper. It's not significantly different than the paper that's in your book. It's green, and it's got some kind of woven junk in it so that, theoretically, a person can't counterfeit it. But it's paper. It doesn't know if you're a priest or a pornographer. Look, it's paper. That's all it is. Nothing less. It's just paper. It doesn't have a conscience. It doesn't know what you are, doesn't know what you do, and doesn't care. It just moves around. That's all.

If money or the movement of money functioned on conscience, there never could be an Enron. There couldn't have been a Jessie James. The money would stop before it got to them. It would put on the brakes. It would speak. It would say, "Wait a minute! You're doing something we don't approve of. We're not coming into your hands." The stuff would work like Matrix movie stuff: "Stop! Go back!" And you wouldn't be able to get it. Money doesn't do that.

It has a different definition of "fairness." It moves to those who do the things that are magnetic to it. If you put a powerful magnet on the tool bench of a good man or the tool bench of a bad man, metal filings will still be drawn across the bench to the magnet. That's its fairness: simple, basic, primal cause and effect.

That doesn't mean you should be a pornographer. I'm not suggesting that. It doesn't mean you should run Enron. I'm not suggesting that. In fact, there are very pragmatic arguments for honesty and integrity and for choosing to produce and market products and services that enrich and improve peoples' lives. What I'm suggesting is you've got to get out of your head that by not doing "bad" things and by doing things that are "good," that alone attracts and multiplies. It doesn't. It may make your next life a better deal. You may be in a cool place instead of a warm place. You may not come back as a toad. Whatever your belief system is about afterlife, it may have impact there. But here and now, there are cause and effect principles of wealth attraction completely separated from virtue.

Wealth Magnet 4
Accepting Your Role and Responsibilities

O h, you're an entrepreneur? Greedy bastard! Surely you know that's what some people think about you and say about you behind your back.

A successful entrepreneur drives down the street in his Rolls-Royce or builds his mansion. If not to his face, then behind his back, many grumble about his greed. But if they hit the mega-millions lottery, they might very well do the same things—most lottery winners do. It's not a moral objection to greed they're expressing. It's the sin of envy.

Too often, achievement, accomplishment, and ambition are defined as greed.

Here's my clarification: greed is attempting to get something for nothing, to take without exchange.

Is getting the most money possible for the goods or services you deliver greed or intelligence? Is it greed or ambition? Are you a better person if you voluntarily get less money than you could for the goods or the services you deliver? No, in fact, you are derelict in your duty as business owner. You have a duty to yourself, your family, your investors, partners, or shareholders, your lenders, your vendors and your customers. That responsibility is to attain the absolute highest and greatest profits possible so you can stay in business successfully to honor every commitment to every one of these constituencies. To settle for anything less than the most is absolute dereliction of the responsibility of business ownership and leadership. To settle for anything less is to leave your business vulnerable, possibly fragile. And you should be fired. Doing this job and honoring your responsibility is a matter of integrity.

Now, here's my question for you: what is your *entrepreneurial responsibility*? What is the entrepreneur's responsibility? What must you do in order to deserve your place on the planet and your success, prosperity, security, and wealth?

A lot of people think your purpose, your responsibility in life, is to provide jobs. You see that reflected in the communities that are busily trying to pass laws, and in some cases suing companies, to keep them from moving or closing, because their responsibility is to provide jobs to the community.

Is your responsibility to provide jobs? I hope you don't think so.

If providing jobs makes your business successful, if adding jobs makes it more successful, that's terrific. But if operating the

NO B.S. Guide to Wealth Attraction for Entrepreneurs 31

business with fewer employees makes it more profitable, then it is your sworn responsibility as its captain to operate it with fewer employees.

A lot of people think your responsibility is to pay taxes.

Personally, I'd be a little happier with my six-figure income tax bill if the IRS sent me pictures of Iraqi citizens and welfare recipients—like when you send money to the starving orphan organization and you get the photograph and a letter once in a while about how they're doing. I think every taxpayer should get some of those and have people assigned to them. So for your money, you've got a picture of these 17 Iraqis, 4 welfare recipients, and this retired guy, and you can put all the people you're supporting up on the refrigerator. And they should all have to write you notes every once in a while to let you know how they're doing. I'd feel better. Wouldn't you?

You have a legal responsibility to pay the minimum taxes required of you.

But your responsibilities as entrepreneur do not include paying any more taxes than the minimum legally required of you. If you can arrange your business structure or affairs differently or relocate your business in order to pay less taxes, it is your sworn responsibility to do so.

Is your responsibility to improve your customers' lives? No, it is not. Now, it's pretty smart to sell them things that, if they use them as you intended, will improve their lives. That's smart. But it's not your responsibility to see that it gets done. Nor should you lose any sleep over the customers who do not use what you sell them to improve their lives.

I had to come to grips with that in my businesses very early on, or I'd have had my wealth attraction severely suppressed. A lot of my wealth has been derived from writing, recording, and publishing information products intended to help people better their attitudes, thinking, skills, businesses, and finances—just like this book. Frankly, a whole lot of what I sell, the shrink-wrap doesn't come off. And you will kill yourself in my business if you worry about making people take off the shrink-wrap. The books never get read. The ideas never get acted on.

Should I feel guilty about the majority who pay their money but then never do anything with what they bought? Should I follow them home and refund their money? When I take a cruise, stay at a top-flight resort, or buy another racehorse, I give no thought to whether the money paying for it came to me from someone who used what they bought or came from someone who has never benefited at all. That's not my responsibility. It is theirs. And the cruise ship company has yet to inquire.

If my client who builds and installs deluxe, premium-priced backyard sheds has a customer who puts the shed in his backyard, never moves the crap out of the garage into the shed, and still can't park the car in the garage or one who moves all of the crap out of the garage into the shed, then restocks the garage with more crap, and still can't park the car in the garage, should my client go out and give them their money back?

Of course not. In fact, he should go out there and sell them a second shed. Sell them garbage removal service. Sell them a how-to-do a garage sale kit. Sell them something.

The entrepreneur's responsibility is this: maximum profit and wealth to his shareholders. If you're the sole shareholder, that's you. Then your responsibility is just to play fair and not lie, cheat, or steal. Integrity for the entrepreneur is optimizing sales, profits, and value in the business he captains.

Just as the boxer who pulls punches in a championship fight lacks integrity, just as the quarterback who does not thoroughly prepare for the Super Bowl game lacks integrity, and just as the lawyer who does not thoroughly prepare for trial lacks integrity, just as the doctor who operates with a hangover lacks integrity, the business owner who pulls his punches also lacks integrity.

Are You "Guilty" of Opportunism?

Shortly after President George W. Bush sent U.S. troops into Iraq, American Greetings Corporation rushed to the presses with a line of greeting cards to be sent to the military in Iraq. They created what they call the romantic ones, like one with a picture of a great-looking babe in a camouflage piece of lingerie, standing next to a bed, with the caption, "I've got some maneuvers to show you when you get home." There are war-themed cards for brothers, for sisters, for fathers, for mothers. The company got massive publicity as a result of this—on *CNN, MSNBC,* and *Entertainment Tonight* and in *USA Today.*

I saw a critical discussion of this line on some talk show. A liberal Hollywood celebrity attempting to launch a career as a political talking head railed about how horrible it was that this company was profiteering on this war. She contended that if, in fact, they are going to sell these things, they should be giving all the money away.

Of course, she, the show, and the network she was appearing on were also opportunists profiteering from exactly the same thing. The "story" of this outrage was their content and their programming. She did not offer to donate her pay for the evening to a charity.

This is an illustration of a position that is very often taken about opportunism. Truth is, everyone is opportunistic. Some are just better at it than others. The homeless beggar who discovers a dumpster filled nightly with exceptionally good leftovers and returns to it each night is an opportunist. If he keeps it secret and does not tell the other homeless folks about it, he's exceptionally opportunistic. I doubt this liberal denouncing the greeting card company would criticize the homeless person or recognize and acknowledge her own opportunism.

What is viewed as opportunism by many is entrepreneurship. That's what it is. Every man's tragedy is somebody else's opportunity. That's commerce.

I have friends and past clients in the fire alarm business. This business wouldn't exist if there weren't fires. You can't sell alarms if people were not having houses burn down around them. If there were no deaths, there'd be no business. In fact, the local sales organizations in this industry very opportunistically target neighborhoods immediately after a local home has caught fire and burnt to the ground.

They position their business as the mission, to protect people and to save lives. That's how they sell what they sell. But their business wouldn't exist if it were not for the tragic problem in the first place.

But here's what's really important. If there weren't really appealing profits in the fire alarm business, the thousands of people whose lives are saved each year by having full-house fire alarm systems would, instead, be crispy critters. The fire alarm sales business is a difficult business. Appointments have to be obtained to visit with people in their homes to discuss a subject no one is voluntarily interested in. Salespeople must be recruited, trained, and managed. This all requires considerable cost, investment, and patience. The salespeople must suffer a lot of rejection and must convince people to accept and act on a threat they prefer to deny. A factory has to exist to manufacture alarms, requiring capital from investors.

None of that can happen without a lot of wealth to be had from this business.

So, the alarm that goes off at 2:00 A.M. tonight, that gets little Debbie and dad, mom, and kitty-cat out of their house alive at 2:11 A.M., immediately before the entire home becomes blazing inferno at 2:14 A.M. is on the wall of their home because a "greedy, opportunistic" fire alarm salesperson was in their home last week and delivered a high-pressure sales presentation with all the passion and persuasiveness he could muster.

So one man's tragedy is another man's opportunity. Entrepreneurship is all about opportunism.

A gas station raises its prices on the Friday before a holiday weekend. Is its proprietor an evil opportunist? What do you think? It's all part and parcel of what he must do in order to achieve maximum success in his business. Because at other times during the calendar year, there are price wars in his neighborhood, and he sells his gas for less than it costs him in order to stay in business. If he's in an extremely competitive environment, he sells his gas at a loss the entire time in order to get repair business into the bays.

There are all sorts of fluctuations in his business. He'd better make maximum profits when the opportunity presents itself, in order to compensate for the times when he can't make any profit at all.

Consider the person who owns a convenience store in the middle of a gang-ridden ghetto where nobody else will open a store. He mostly sells to people who can't get 20 miles away to the nearest supermarket; therefore, he sells at double what you could buy the same products for if you could get to the supermarket 20 miles away. Is he an evil opportunist? Well, would you open a store there? If his store's not there, how do locals get anything at all? His risk is enormously higher than the guy with the supermarket 20 miles away. Every time he walks into the store, there's a very real chance somebody's going to walk in the door and blow his head off, or try. His theft rate is probably 400% or 500% worse than the supermarket 20 miles away. For assuming all of that added risk, shouldn't he be an opportunist?

Getting all this stuff about greed and opportunism out of your head is critical. As an entrepreneur, you have a particular role in the world. You are a vitally important economic force. You have certain real responsibilities you need to embrace. The illegitimate responsibilities others would impose on you must be rejected. Embrace the rewards you deserve.

Wealth Magnet 5
No Fear

I s there a "dirty little secret" behind many wealthy entrepreneurs' success stories?

Yes, but probably not any that would instantly pop to most peoples' minds. Some people think it's luck, who they knew, rich relatives, or disreputable behavior such as somehow taking ruthless advantage of others, climbing to wealth by stepping on others. It is none of those things.

It is a past bankruptcy. Or at least a huge failure and wipeout and near-bankruptcy experience.

I've personally worked closely with nearly 200 first-generation, from-scratch millionaire and multimillionaire entrepreneurs.

Bankruptcy Alumni

A partial list of famous and successful people who have gone through bankruptcy:

- P.T. Barnum
- David Buick (founder, Buick Motors)
- Walt Disney
- James Folger (founder, Folgers Coffee)
- Henry Ford
- Conrad Hilton
- J.C. Penney
- Sam Walton
- William Fox (founder, 20th Century Fox Film Corp.)
- H. J. Heinz
- Frank Lloyd Wright

Nearly half have gone bankrupt before ultimately, finally achieving lasting success and wealth. A significant number of legendary entrepreneurs have bankruptcies in their pasts. This is true of historical figures as well as contemporary ones. The incredible commonality among successful entrepreneurs is having been broke or formerly gone through bankruptcy.

There are reasons.

For one thing, *entrepreneurial success and wealth creation, as well as wealth attraction, require a willingness to risk and experience failure*

*and the emotional resiliency to recover from it quickly, decisively, pas-
sionately, and persistently.* Hardly anybody gets to success via a
straight line. So the past bankruptcy is revealing of this trait, may
have been instrumental in the development of this trait, or both.

But more importantly, in my opinion, bankruptcy is one of
those profound experiences that leads the entrepreneur to full
and complete understanding of just how replaceable money is.
When you experience a bankruptcy, as I have, you feel as if life
is over, that you'll never recover, that you'll forever have a big
red "B" on your forehead, that you'll never get credit. Then
when you discover none of that is true and that money is readily
available, wealth replaceable more quickly and easily than the
first time around, the light bulb comes on to full power. It's a
huge "ah-ha!" and a giant "Well, I'll be damned." From the
moment of that realization forward, your fears about money are
permanently banished and erased. What you feared was fatal
turned out to be less than a flesh wound. Now you can't be
scared again.

> **Fears about money inhibit
> your wealth attraction powers.**
>
> **Absence of fears about money
> releases your full
> wealth attraction power.**

Everyone who is anyone with achievement and wisdom counsels us against fear. Jesus Christ counseled against fear. Pope John Paul III counseled against fear. Earl Nightingale, the pioneer in self-improvement pointed out that most the things we worry endlessly about never occur except in our own negative imaginations. Napoleon Hill wrote in his classic *Laws of Success* about the ghosts of fear. The President he wrote speeches for goaded America out of the Depression and famously said, "We have nothing to fear but fear itself."

Who's Been Fired?

Larry King, Bill Belechick, Lee Iacocca. Lance Armstrong was fired from the French team Cofids in 1997 after he began treatment for testicular cancer. In 2005, he won the Tour de France for the 7th time. Katie Couric was fired from CNN after the network's president said he never wanted to see her face on TV again. Bob Woodward was fired from the *Washington Post* and told to get more experience. He was rehired, broke the Watergate story, and was awarded the Pulitizer Prize.

—From the book *We Got Fired—And It's the Best Thing That Ever Happened to Us*, by Harvey Mackay, author of *Swim with the Sharks*

Every client I've ever had who has made a fear-based business decision has later regretted it. Every time we say no to fear, we win.

It's important to understand that fear is learned. We are born with fears of falling, loud unknown noises, and snakes. Otherwise, God sends us here completely free of fear. We learn our fears from other humans. We are conditioned to be fearful by what we hear and observe as children, by the influences of other fearful adults we associate with. The irrational nature of most fears is well illustrated by the fact that more people fear public speaking than fear debilitating illness or death. More people fear airplane travel than automobile travel even though statistically air travel is infinitely safer.

It is my observation and conviction that more people are controlled and inhibited by their fears about money than by any other kind of fear. People fear not having it, but they also fear being changed by having it. They fear making poor decisions

> When you jettison all money fears, you instantaneously become magnetic to money. I now believe your bank balance reflects the ratio of fear vs. confidence you have about money.

about it. They fear running out of it before they die. They fear losing it most of all. The best people, and even the wealthiest, still have a whole lot of emotional baggage and b.s. connected to money in their closets!

After my bankruptcy, which I feared would be fatal, I quickly discovered it was a mere bump in the road, and my fears were replaced with a rapidly growing confidence. Many years later, my wife and I divorced after 22 years of marriage. One half of all the wealth accumulated in the prior ten years or so, a considerable amount, marched out the door with her. You could say it was at least 10 years of wealth. I easily replaced it in less than 18 months. I nearly doubled it in 24 months.

All of my prior experiences, including what I'd learned from my bankruptcy recovery, proved to be worth far more than the actual money that moved out with her. I had zero fears about the loss of the money, about the difficulty of replacing it, or about it having any adverse impact on my life or lifestyle. I just strolled over to the wall, adjusted the thermostat on my wealth attraction powers and let the coffers refill, then overflow.

This is not to suggest license to behave recklessly or foolishly with your wealth. Waste, imprudence, and irresponsibility is almost always punished because such behavior is repulsive to money. But confidence magnetically attracts it because confidence reflects real understanding and everyone and everything is attracted to understanding.

Consider an analogy, something you once did not understand, found incredibly difficult if not impossible to do, and hoped you would not encounter or have to deal with. Often there's some single, simple "trick" that changes everything. For example, if you attempt to assemble difficult jigsaw puzzles with a zillion pieces and you don't know that it helps enormously to build the outside four sides first; you may be stymied and frustrated until somebody takes pity on you and shows you that trick. The "Oh, now I understand!" moment is wonderful, isn't it? Well, here's the trick about money: understanding that it is available in unlimited supply and readily replaceable changes everything.

Wealth Magnet 6
No Excuses

Few people are attracted to whiners, complainers, excuse-makers, or wimps. Hanging out with a victim is not appealing to most reasonably sane people. Who wants to be around or involved with an emotional cripple? The person in the victim shirt tends to wear out his welcome early—as he should. This thinking, these beliefs, and his behavior are even more repellant to money and wealth than they are to other people.

In *No B.S. Business Success*, I explain that power is derived from taking responsibility, weakness from disavowing it. Here, I will add that wealth is attracted by taking responsibility, repelled by disavowing it.

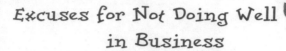

Excuses for Not Doing Well in Business

- "Everybody in my city buys by price."
- "Nobody in my town uses credit cards."
- "Everybody in my town is cheap."
- "There's a giant advertiser in my town."
- "I never get the good leads."
- "It's the time of year."
- "There's already too many doohickeys in my town."
- "What I do is so unique, nobody understands it."
- "It's the economy, it's my spouse, my staff . . ."

It is interesting and a bit frustrating to me to watch the debate over the gap between worker and top executive compensation in corporate America play out, especially the strident complaints about extraordinarily high CEO pay. What the complaints ignore is the responsibility differential. The pay differential is admittedly extreme, but the responsibility differential is still more extreme. An automobile manufacturing company is a good example. The company makes, ships, sells, and delivers 450,000 dangerously defective cars, which must now be recalled. This costs the company and its shareholders millions of dollars, putting it at competitive disadvantage in the marketplace and furthering the economic damage, and harming the ability of the dealers and salespeople to make their livings as well. The worker on the assembly line and the factory supervisors get off scot free, with zero responsibility. They do not need to give back any of their pay or perks; they go home that Friday unaffected and unconcerned, without penalty. The CEO winds up with all the responsibility. He must answer to his board, the shareholders, Wall Street, the news media, the dealers, the customers, and the insurance company. He does not go home that Friday unaffected and unconcerned, not by a long shot. Yes, he has a large income and stock options. He has wealth and he has power. But he also has enormous responsibility.

The two are not coincidentally or incidentally linked. They are, instead, cause and effect. In most cases, he has risen, more accurately climbed to his CEO post over time, by the act of taking on more and more and more responsibility. Others have chosen not to seek and take on more responsibility. (Key word: chosen.) In fact, most shirk it, hide from it. The CEO's power and wealth has flowed to him as he has reached out and grabbed more and more responsibility. He has also taken on greater and greater risk. (Ask Martha Stewart or Bernie Ebbers or Richard Shusky.) It is his willingness to take on the responsibility that has brought him his wealth.

In the world of the entrepreneur, there is even clearer correlation between the taking on of responsibility and risk and the attraction of opportunity and wealth. If, as the saying goes, you can't stand the heat, stay out of the kitchen. But if you do, you ought not begrudge the goodies gobbled up by the big lads willing to stand in the fire.

As an entrepreneur, you are going to screw up. And you are going to have bad things happen on your watch that you actually

Individuals' ACTUAL Stated Reasons for not Getting to Work on Time

Woody Allen said that half of success is showing up. The other half is showing up on time. These are peoples' excuses for being unable to show up on time.

- "Sometimes my car won't start."

- "The damned bus driver comes early."

- "I can't hear the alarm clock."

- "The dog hides my shoes."

- "I just can't get going. I'm not a morning person."

- "My mother was never a morning person." (It's mom's fault I can't get to work on time.)

- "It's unfair to ask somebody to be there at exactly the same time every morning."

had no hand in or feel you couldn't possibly prevent. That's a given. What's important to understand is that the world watches and responds to the way you handle these situations. If you blame others, blame circumstances, or offer up excuses, you telegraph weakness. If you step up, accept responsibility, offer no excuses, and roll up your sleeves and work, you telegraph strength and command respect. With excuse-making, you may obtain some sympathy and pity but at the price of respect. And wealth is never transferred based on pity. It moves based on respect. Wealth attraction power has a great deal to do with self-respect and the respect of others, and that has a great deal to do with your acceptance, even your embrace, of responsibility.

In 2005, Bill Rancic spoke at one of my Inner Circle Member conferences. You know Bill because he was the first season winner on Donald Trump's TV show, *The Apprentice*. Bill was a very successful entrepreneur pre-Trump and had many valuable insights and experiences to share from his other businesses as well as his year with The Donald. One such story was about one of his earliest businesses. As a kid, he cleaned and readied boats in a resort area for the seasonal arrival of their owners. Things

Losers are wealthy with excuses. They have moth-eaten, empty wallets and heads full of excuses. This is not an enviable wealth. An abundance of excuses guarantees a paucity of money. If excuses roll willingly from a person's tongue, it's certain money does not flow easily into his pockets. I've often said I can estimate a person's bank balance if he'll tell me about the books he reads and the people he hangs out with. But it's even easier to accurately estimate his bank balance if I hear the excuses he makes. The habit of excuse making is the worst of all habits.

went horribly awry, and as he said, most kids would have cut and run or blamed the circumstances involved. He did not. He took an arguably unjustified 100% of the responsibility for himself, with the direct result of impressing and keeping all his customers, but the more important, if indirect, result was strengthening his overall wealth attraction power.

If you remember the wonderful Pink Panther movies with Peter Sellers, you'll remember his Asian houseboy, who he paid to attack him without warning, to keep him on his toes. I've been told by good authority that the boxer Mike Tyson once hired a man to walk behind him saying, "You the man, Mike, you the man." (There's a clue to how Tyson could zip through $100 million and be broke.) A fine investment would be hiring a big, strong guy to walk around with you for a month carrying a stout baseball bat and every time you voiced an excuse, hauling off and knocking you into next week. I imagine you'll be unwilling to make that investment, so instead, you might try keeping a little notebook in your pocket to list every excuse you catch yourself making for the next month, as well as every excuse you get from anyone else. Awareness automatically improves performance, so just the act of keeping the diary and stopping whatever you're doing each time you proffer an excuse will have positive impact. Getting whacked silly by the strong man with a Louisville Slugger would have more impact, but admittedly the side effects are problematic.

If you recall the cartoon character Popeye, you'll remember that he pumped up his strength and power when needed by gulping down a can or two of spinach. I think of that as a visualization analogy, for the entrepreneur, responsibility is spinach. If you want to turn on wealth attraction power, gulp down some more.

There are no victims. Only volunteers.

—LEE MILTEER

AUTHOR OF *SUCCESS IS AN INSIDE JOB*

WWW.LEEMILTEER.COM

". . . in 1969, only one year out of graduate school, I had the good fortune to work for W. Clement Stone. He was a self-made multimillionaire worth $600 million at the time. Stone was also America's premier success guru. He was the publisher of *Success* magazine, author of *The Success System That Never Fails*, and co-author with Napoleon Hill of *Success Through a Positive Mental Attitude*.

When I was completing my first week's orientation, Mr. Stone asked me if I took 100% responsibility for my life. 'I think so,' I responded."

"This is a yes or no question, young man. You either do or you don't."

"Well, I guess I'm not sure."

"Have you ever blamed anyone for any circumstance in your life? Have you ever complained about anything?"

"Uh...yeah...I guess I have."

"Don't guess. Think."

"Yes, I have."

"Okay then. That means you don't take 100% responsibility for your life. Taking 100% responsibility means you acknowledge that you create everything that happens to you. It means you understand that you are the cause of all your experience. If you want to be truly successful, and I know you do, then you will have to give up blaming and complaining and take total responsibility for your life—that means all your results, your successes and your failures. This is a prerequisite for creating a life of success . . . . You see, Jack, if you realize that you have created your current conditions, then you can uncreate them and recreate them at will. Do you understand that? Are you willing to take 100% responsibility for your life?"

"Yes, sir, I am!—and I did."

—JACK CANFIELD, *THE SUCCESS PRINCIPLES*,
CO-AUTHOR, *CHICKEN SOUP FOR THE SOUL*
WWW.THESUCCESSPRINCIPLES.COM, WWW.JACKCANFIELD.COM

Wealth Magnet 7
Speak Money

Most people speak lack, poverty, inadequacy, doubt, and fear.

You have to be careful about the vocabulary you use because every word or thought, spoken or written, if inner-directed, constitutes programming, instructions to your subconscious mind. It is overly simplistic to believe that what you say in your head (think) and speak out loud manifests. The title of Napoleon Hill's most famous book *Think and Grow Rich* is slightly misleading; more accurately it should be *How to Think to Grow Rich*. Thought alone will not override behavior or certain physical realities and circumstances. However, it is accurate to say that the way you think about money and the language you use about money matters a great deal. It is revealing of the programming your subconscious is actually being directed by, and it is accumulating programming it is trying to respond to. Further, your spoken words convey your relative comfort and confidence or discomfort and fear about money to others. Any sales professional can tell you that prospects "smell fear" like animals. This is not superstition on their part. Experienced sales pros know it is infinitely harder to make the sale you desperately feel you must make than the sale that doesn't matter much one way or the other. Professional negotiators all know that the person who wants it least has the power. These are analogies to all movement of money. Money is naturally attracted to the person most confident and comfortable about it.

People tend to transfer their money to these same people. When you are talking to others, there's text and subtext, heard by others' conscious and subconscious minds. When you say that you just don't "feel good" about somebody or that your "intuition" tells you not to trust or do business with somebody, it's your subconscious processing impressions from sight, sound, and the other senses, searching its files for past information and experiences. You can't actually enunciate why you feel as you do. You just do. You might not consciously realize that when you're around Joe, he often talks in terms of lack, poverty, failure, and fear, so you do not want to buy from him, invest with him, or otherwise be involved with him. But that may very well be what has occurred within your subconscious.

For all these reasons, what you speak about money matters.

As an example, consider the term "hard-earned dollars." You recognize the term, don't you? Hard-earned dollars. You probably heard your parents say it. Your friends may say it. You may say it, or some variation of it, without ever considering its true meaning. If you translate it to programming, it is that money is very hard to get. You get money only through difficult and unpleasant work. If money somehow arrives without being connected to hard work, there's something wrong with it. It's tainted or toxic. It's incorrect and dishonorable to get it easily.

Now consider the phrase "easy money." For most people, this is "bad." The perception is that "easy money" is somehow tainted, dirty, undeserved. The perception is that the person always seeking "easy money" is a lazy bum or a fool.

What a barrier! This is a tall, wide, thick wall that prevents entrepreneurs from looking for or seeing many great opportunities in their own businesses lying there within easy reach. I think this explains why a pair of fresh, expert eyes like mine can so easily and frequently see unexploited opportunities in others' businesses. It's not just that the owner of the business is too close to the forest to see the trees. There's a wall he can't see through boxing him in.

What a barrier! If things start to get easy, if money starts flowing in faster in bigger sums than ever before, the entrepreneur will subconsciously reject it and engage in all manner of self-sabotage to slow the unjust flow.

The fact is, there's no reason money has to be hard to earn or earned in hard ways. I've taught thousands of entrepreneurs how to earn much larger incomes more easily. Take my client, Dr. Paul Searby, who was barely earning a living working 50 hour weeks as a dentist. He now earns as much in two months as he used to earn all year, working only one day a week teaching dentists how to create second businesses with dental assistant schools. Or consider my Platinum Member Yanik Silver, who has developed an internet marketing business bringing in millions of dollars that he operates via his laptop from anywhere in the world in just a couple hours a day. He seems to constantly be on vacation somewhere, yet he began barely able to turn on a computer. Or take my client and Gold/VIP Member, Chet Rowland, who owns a "grunge business," a large pest control company. Thanks to his extraordinarily comprehensive and effective business systems, he operates profitably, grows every year, and provides himself with over a million dollars a year even though he goes to his office only once or twice a month. Chet uses some of his free time to make hundreds of thousands of dollars buying preconstruction high rise condos in Florida and flipping them before they are built.

Consider the real estate business. The typical real estate agent does a lot of manual labor prospecting work to finally get an appointment to make a listing presentation to get the right to sell a house, then does a lot of manual labor showing that house to possible buyers, etc., etc., etc., to possibly make a $10,000.00 or $20,000.00 commission. Together, Craig Proctor and Ron Romano at Automated Marketing Solutions, two clients of mine, literally reinvented the way that business is done by using a special type of advertising: toll-free phone numbers and recorded messages, web sites, and other technology to slash the manual labor by half, so that the agent makes money more easily and can make twice as much money from the same number of work hours. As I am writing this book, Craig Proctor is again reinventing the business to further alter the ratio between "hard work" and "income."

Another client of mine, Rob Minton, has succeeded with his own total, dramatic reinvention of the real estate business, focusing exclusively on working with investors. So, a real estate agent works with 5 clients who each buy 10 homes rather than 50 clients who each buy 1 home. He keeps clients in place buying year after year, some even paying "membership dues" to be in the real estate agent's "club" and be permitted to buy.

Similarly, for real estate investors, my Gold/VIP Member, Matt Gillogly has invented a powerful direct-mail program that brings motivated property sellers to investors as if an assembly line were in place leading to their doors! Or consider the insurance business, where my client, Dean Cipriano has virtually eliminated the need for "cold prospecting" by sales professionals—he actually delivers them all the qualified leads they can handle on a silver platter. Or, in the mortgage industry, my clients Tracy Tolleson and Scott Tucker have, in different ways, made it possible for the mortgage professional to make a high six-figure income working less than 30 hours a week, no weekends, cellphone turned off evenings and weekends, and no manual labor prospecting.

All these people are living "easy money," or at least "easier money," and showing others how to distance themselves from "hard earned dollars."

Even consider me. In 1996, I earned a million dollars from speaking, which required nearly constant travel. I delivered over 60 presentations during the year and did the writing, publishing, and selling of information products at every speech. It required a staff person to process all the orders, and a vendor to ship products. In 2004, I earned a million dollars from coaching just five small groups of entrepreneurs who come and meet with me. They require only 26 days of meetings in my home cities plus 16 days of talking on the phone, often while sitting in the sun on my backyard deck or in my big leather recliner in my library. Counting travel days and speaking days, in 1996 it required more than 200 days to earn what only 42 days provided in 2004. And these were considerably easier, less strenuous, and less stressful days. This shift involved procedural changes in my business, changes in strategy, but also, of equal importance, continuous improvement of my thinking, understanding, and even imaginings about money. In 2006, I will retain that same income from only 34 days.

Breaking free of the Work-Money Link has not been easy for me. I was raised to have enormous respect for the work ethic. My youth experiences taught me that money is hard earned and earned hard. Shaking that view, replacing that thinking is no simple trick. But that link is an illusion, not a reality.

This is not to suggest that I don't work or that you shouldn't. In fact, I think work of some kind is necessary for sound mental and physical health. But there is work, and then there is work. My Platinum Member Ron LeGrand's motto is "The Less I Do, The More I Make," which is subject to misinterpretation. It is meant as a variation on the "work smarter, not harder" theme. Personally, I work at working on my terms, on things that I enjoy involvement with, and on high yield opportunities and tasks, and I coach others to do the same. I am all about finding ways to make things easier, not harder. To do more with less. To gain leverage. But if you think and speak the belief of "hard-earned dollars," you reinforce a barrier to doing any of these things.

"Hard-earned dollars" is just one example of hundreds of negative, limiting statements routinely thought and said about money. They are all bricks strengthening and reinforcing the wall between you and easy attraction of maximum wealth.

Do you have kids? How many times in the last month did you explain to the kids that money doesn't grow on trees?

Where's that come from? Maybe you've become your father. Maybe you are simply repeating what you've always heard. It's been programmed in. And now, at a particular point in life, you are regurgitating it and spitting it back out with no thought about what it's doing to you or what it's doing to the person that you're saying it to. But when you say this, what belief system is it communicating and reinforcing?

I am not for spoiling kids, but that's another discussion for another time and place. For now, let's keep the harsh spotlight focused on you. When something like that spews out of your mouth, it came from somewhere. It came from your own mind, your subconscious, your belief system, the recordings that play inside your head. Whatever you say about money is simultaneously revealing and reinforcing.

There is a language used by wealth-attracting entrepreneurs. I hear it all the time because I hang out and work with them most of my work life. I've been surrounded by them for years. They speak one language; the outside world speaks another. I'm not going to hand you a vocabulary list here and suggest you try memorizing it or reading positive affirmations 20 times a day from 3-by-5 cards. That can be useful, but it is a tiny piece of this puzzle, and overly simplistic. Trying to use a vocabulary list won't cut it. The language has to be an honest, natural reflection of your beliefs about money and wealth. Everything in this book has to come together and support the changes you choose to make in your own belief system.

But make no mistake, what you speak matters. And you can attract more wealth more easily by speaking the language of wealth.

Wealth Magnet 8
Be Somebody

B e a famous somebody. Like it or not, we live in a celebrity-obsessed culture, a celebrity-driven marketplace.

In recent years, my clients in the seminar and conference business have dramatically increased attendance, total on-site revenues, or both by adding celebrity speakers including Donald Trump and Dr. Phil, to their events. And for nine years I spoke on the biggest seminar tour ever, 25 to 29 cities a year, to audiences of 10,000 to 30,000, with speakers like former Presidents Ford, Reagan, and Bush; Generals Colin Powell and Norman Schwartzkopf; Larry King, Bill Cosby, and dozens more from Hollywood, sports, politics and business. Stadiums were filled for business seminars as if they were rock concerts because of the drawing power of these celebrities. My client of many years, the Guthy-Renker Corporation, changed the infomercial industry forever when it began using celebrity hosts and testimonials in its TV infomercials. Even *Forbes* magazine now publishes an annual issue about the wealthiest and most influential celebrities, and it sells just as well as its annual issue about the richest business leaders. No matter your market—CEOs or ditch-diggers, young or old, poor or super-affluent—they are influenced by and attracted to celebrity.

So it is smart to make yourself into a celebrity.

Not necessarily the kind who appears on *Oprah* or the cover of *People*, but a celebrity within your own business sphere, your own market, whether that's defined geographically, demographically, by particular industry or profession, or otherwise. The smaller the universe, the easier it is to be a celebrity. Arnold Schwarzenegger was first a celebrity in the niche world of bodybuilding from which he extracted a great deal of wealth before the general public was even aware of his existence. Many of my clients are famous celebrities in their own industries, quite likely to be stopped and asked for their autographs or to collect a crowd at their industry conventions, yet you would neither recognize their faces nor know their names.

At a local level, it is relatively easy for a businessperson to achieve celebrity status, in large part merely by making himself a focal point of all his advertising. In Edmonton, Canada, my Gold/VIP Member Dr. Barry Lycka is a bona fide celebrity. When he offers an open seminar or special event, hundreds attend. He has long featured himself in extensive newspaper, TV, and direct-mail advertising for both his practice and his spa. My client

Darin Garman, a commercial real estate broker and developer, has attracted investors to Iowa real estate from all over the world by making it all about him, and making himself into a celebrity with his "Former Iowa Prison Guard Discovers . . ." story. In Redding, California, Bob Higgins is a celebrity. If you stopped 20 people on the street at random, at least 1 would know who Bob is. And his business is house painting! (You can see and read about some of their highly effective advertising in my book *No B.S. Direct Marketing for NON-Direct Marketing Businesses.*)

Local celebrity can lead to national celebrity. Dr. Robert Kotler, a Beverly Hills cosmetic surgeon and one-time client of mine, began making himself a "celebrity doctor" with local advertising of his self-published book, *The Consumers' Guide to Cosmetic Surgery* and then with Los Angeles media appearances. Recently, he was a featured doctor on *Dr. 90210*, a reality TV series aired nationally on the E network.

Certainly within your own clientele, it is easy to be a celebrity, and being one will improve customer or client retention, spending, and referrals. To your own clientele, you build your own celebrity status through self-aggrandizement, self-promotion, and association with celebrities. Any and every photo of you with a celebrity has real value to you.

Consider my client Daniel Frishberg, a highly skilled and respected investment analyst, managing millions of dollars for clients. Like many financial advisors, he utilized his own bought-and-paid-for radio call-in program in his local market (San Antonio, Texas) to attract clients. But unlike most, he dared to go after all sorts of nationally famous celebrities and experts to be interviewed on his little, local radio program. And he got them, from Henry Kissinger and Alan Greenspan to Roger Moore

(James Bond) and Pat Sajak (*Wheel of Fortune*). Frishberg's little radio show was a star-studded cavalcade. And the stardust rubbed off, making him far more attractive and interesting to more people and to more affluent people, as well as to other advertisers to subsidize his program. Before you could say "Hollywood," his paid-for weekly radio program morphed into a daily real radio program, and then went on to air in both San Antonio and the much bigger market of Houston. Recently, he and a group of investors bought the whole radio station in Houston that airs his program!

Simply by surrounding himself with celebrities, Daniel Frishberg made himself a celebrity in the eyes of his investor clients and prospective clients. This strategy of becoming a celebrity by surrounding yourself with them is actually very reliable and often repeated. My one-time client, Peter Lowe, for whom I consulted and spoke at more than 200 events, did this same thing for himself as a speaker. My client Guthy-Renker did this for Tony Robbins with the series of TV infomercials, each one featuring a better collection of celebrity hosts and testimonials. I, too, have very consciously applied this strategy over many years.

Be an Expert Somebody

Expert status is very magnetic. Fortunately, it is a self-created, self-manufactured asset.

The great success educator Earl Nightingale said you could make yourself a world class expert in most fields simply by studying every available resource for an hour a day for just a year. I took him seriously. I made myself into a top expert in the field of direct marketing entirely through self study, with no academic or experience qualifications whatsoever, in less than three years and began charging high fees from the very beginning. I have also successfully positioned myself as a marketing expert in several different fields. For example, well over 10,000 chiropractors and dentists have attended my practice-building seminars, bought my books and courses on practice marketing, and have been in my coaching programs. I built the largest seminar and publishing company serving these professions in the early '80s. I've been hired to speak for five different major practice building companies as well as state dental and chiropractic associations. Although I was once named "Practice Guru of the Year" by a major trade journal in dentistry, I'm neither a chiropractor nor a dentist.

I am fond of a quote I got from fellow direct response copywriter John Francis Tighe, "In the land of the blind, the one-eyed man is king." If you know more about "x" than your intended clientele, you ARE an expert!

Obviously, everybody prefers working with experts. This is especially true as you climb up the affluency ladder*. But really, everybody prefers dealing with an expert if and when they can. If you suffer from blinding headaches, and you can get to the doctor who wrote *The Official Guide to Drug-Free Headache Relief*, who has a newspaper column about headaches you've seen, and who's on the radio, you would rather go see him about your problem than any other "ordinary" doctor. This is the reason that I worked with experts to create *Dentistry for Diabetics*, a program that educates and certifies one dentist per area in working with diabetic patients—giving him a practice-building asset worth hundreds of thousands of dollars a year.** In essence, specialization, even if self-declared, raises your expert status.

*My friend Elsom Eldridge has written a fantastic book on this subject, *How to be the Obvious Expert!* See www.obvious-expert.com.

I edit a special newsletter entirely devoted to the subject of marketing to the affluent and mass affluent. You can obtain information at www.dankennedy.com.

**For information about DDS for Diabetics, fax 602-269-3113.

Experts encounter less fee or price resistance, so they can usually charge premium prices and enjoy above-average profit margins. If they choose, they can derive greater income from fewer clients or customers. Because my client and Gold/VIP Member Dr. Charles Martin is an expert in "longevity dentistry" or "whole health dentistry" as well as world class cosmetic dentistry, he can attract patients from all over the country as well as his home city of Richmond, Virginia. He can have cases accepted by patients at fees of $40,000.00 to $70,000.00—while most "ordinary" cosmetic dentists struggle to get one-fourth those fees for the same amount of work. Because my client Darin Garman is an expert in profitable, "peace of mind investing" exclusively in heartland-of-America apartment buildings, he can attract investors from all over the world as well as dominate his local market in Iowa, charge an access fee and monthly membership fee just to be permitted to purchase properties from him, and never, never, never discount commissions. Because my Gold/VIP Member Mark Ijlal offers training, seminars, coaching, and services only to Michigan residents investing in Michigan real estate, he commands a premium price for every service if compared to all other seminars, coaching, and services for all real estate investors. Because my Gold/VIP Member Bill Hammond's elder law practice specializes in working with families with a senior with Alzheimer's, his fees are at the top of the pyramid, mandatorily packaged and not available for cafeteria purchase, and rarely questioned. Of course, you may think you are not in a profession that lends itself to expert status. My contention is that every business does. I could tell you very similar stories about carpet cleaners, lawn and garden companies, auto repair shops, and even an industrial tarp manufacturer, positioned as experts and specialists, prospering from carefully chosen target markets and selling their goods and services for 5 to 25 times their industry norms.

Wealth Magnet 9
Be Somewhere

I n *the midst of one of his dark periods, when the news media* was filled with stories of his financial demise, Donald Trump talks about feeling like just staying hidden at home but instead strapping on his tuxedo and going to an important gala—because he knew he could not possibly gain by staying home. At a time, some 25 years or so ago, when I was captain of a company everyone in its industry knew to be in deep and dire financial circumstances, I considered skipping that year's convention. But I didn't. It might have been less stressful, less embarrassing, and more comfortable to stay home. But I couldn't possibly gain doing that. I went. I put myself in a place where it was at least possible that good, productive, profitable things could happen, and they did.

> *Wealth won't find you if you are at home slouched on— or hiding under—the couch.*

Hopefully, you aren't in the upside-down financial condition I was, or Donald Trump was, at the abovementioned times. But regardless of your circumstances, you have to make a point of putting yourself in places where opportunity can occur. My father passed on a pair of cuff links to me with the letters: YCDBSOYA. They stand for: You Can't Do Business Sitting On Your Ass.

Although this refers to personal movement and placement, such as the meetings, conferences, cocktail parties, and community events you attend and make yourself visible at, it also goes far beyond that. As example, consider this book and the other 14 books I have written and had published.* For more than 14 years, I have been on bookstore shelves without interruption. I have worked hard to make that happen. Why? I can assure you not for the royalty income paid to me as an author; that represents less than 2% of my income. I want to be on those bookshelves because people discover me there, people who might never discover me otherwise. They become Inner Circle

> *A list of my other books appears on page 278. You can also preview samples chapters and excerpts of many of these books at www.nobs books.com.

Members and newsletter subscribers, attend seminars, become private clients, or bring me other opportunities. Being there on bookstore shelves has both directly and indirectly enriched me by millions of dollars. I can specifically identify more than a dozen long-term clients who have each spent between $100,000.00 and $300,000.00 with me. I have been sought out for speaking engagements purely because a corporate executive bought and read one of my books. For me, being somewhere includes being on bookstore shelves, being in this book which is now in your office or home.

That does not mean you must write a book. It is example of the wealth attraction power of being somewhere. Because the most important words in the above paragraph are "discover me" and "sought out." This is marketing by attraction.

Being somewhere for the local insurance agent or financial planner, for example, might mean speaking to local groups of dentists, chiropractors, M.D.s, and other high income professionals. Creating and mailing a good, informative, expert, position-enhancing newsletter on financial matters to a targeted list of such prospects every month. Appearing regularly on a local radio show. Serving on the board of an important charity. Almost any entrepreneur can be somewhere via speaking, writing, publishing, and networking. Even serving, carefully chosen to facilitate the right people taking notice and ultimately seeking you out for advice and information or bringing you new opportunities, can work.

Wealth Magnet 10
Do Something

My friend and master copywriter Gary Halbert's saying is, "Motion beats meditation." It would probably amaze a lot of people if they knew the inside story of a lot of "rags to riches" entrepreneurs' lives as I do, to discover that just about the only reason for their meteoric success was simply getting into motion, before they were ready.

Some years ago, I had an opportunity to spend a day with Lee Iacocca in my consulting work, and I was thrilled to do so. I had long studied him, his business methods, and his personal behavior. I often tell the entrepreneurs I coach about how highly Iacocca prizes decisiveness and action, maybe best illustrated by his story of the rebirth of the convertible at the financially troubled Chrysler. Factory workers caught him walking around and suggested that one of the cars would make a great convertible. He told them to get a blow torch, cut the roof off, let him drive it around and see how people reacted. And the rest, as they say, is history. The relaunch of the convertible by Chrysler probably attracted more media and public attention and brought more money to Chrysler at a faster pace than any other idea ever acted on in its history. All because there was that rare CEO in place who heard a good idea and immediately acted on it. No design committees, no focus groups, no endless meetings of engineers, no long delayed prototype. A blowtorch.

In 2005, for the monthly tele-seminar series I produce for my Inner Circle Members, I had an opportunity to meet and interview another entrepreneur-author I've long studied and admired, Robert Ringer. You may know him from his most famous best-selling book *Winning Through Intimidation,* recently republished as *To Be or Not To Be Intimidated.* I rank it as one of the ten most influential books I have ever read and credit it with directing me to my practice of "Takeaway Selling" described in a companion to this book, *No B.S. Sales Success.* In 2005, I interviewed Mr. Ringer about his newer book *Action!: Nothing Happens Until Something Moves.* And I said on the tele-seminar, if you never read the book, but merely propped it up where you saw its cover everyday, you'd profit. Its title tells you exactly how so many of us attract abundant opportunity and wealth. *Movement.*

I often say if poor people knew how shockingly ordinary millionaires were, there'd be a lot more millionaires. One of the biggest erroneous ideas in the way of poor people getting rich is that the rich are somehow smarter or possess some "magic gene" that separates them from the masses in terms of aptitude or capability. Nothing could be further from the truth. I work very closely, day in, day out, with over 100 millionaire and multimillionaire entrepreneurs, and I assure you, they aren't that much smarter than the clerk at the corner convenience store. I have clients personally earning millions of dollars a year who forget to put on their shoes when they leave the house, have walked through the screen door on the front of my house, are woefully dysfunctional managers, are incredibly disorganized, are slow readers, can't do math, etc. In fact, one, who has built a national chain of tax preparation offices serving hundreds of thousands of clients, can't add two numbers together without a calculator and couldn't decipher a financial statement if you put a gun against his head. The richest real estate investor I work with was a car mechanic, another a prison guard. And frankly, in terms of total, overall work ethic, these folks don't shine either. But there is one thing they all do, that the vast majority of the population doesn't.

In *Action!*, Robert Ringer wrote, "I have always believed that the difference between success and failure, in any area of life, is not nearly as great as most people might suspect." I not only agree, I have abundant proof from the more than 100 "from-scratch"

> *The act of taking action is, in and of itself, a magnet for opportunity and wealth.*

millionaires I've worked with, from their stumbling beginnings to their present wealth, celebrity, expert credibility, and achievements.

The "little" difference is the subject of Ringer's book: these people take action.*

> *Free: You can hear a replay of the teleseminar featuring my interview with Robert Ringer, author of *Action!* online at www.nobsbooks.com.
>
> I co-authored *The New Psycho-Cybernetics*, an updated version of Dr. Maltz' original work *Psycho-Cybernetics*. The book is available in bookstores and from online booksellers; additional information is at www.psycho-cybernetics.com.

You've undoubtedly seen, in many movies, the guns with heat-seeking technology that make the person trying to hide appear in neon red or green as he generates body heat while moving through the dark jungle. You've heard of heat-seeking missiles. There's a similar effect with action and wealth. *Wealth seeks movement.*

Over the years, I've found that just about everybody has at least one really good idea, skill, or talent that could translate to prosperity and success. I once briefly dated a divorced mother with three young kids who worked in a low-wage factory job, barely staying one day ahead of bills. I discovered she occasionally found time to paint—and my jaw dropped when I saw the paintings. I own racehorses, and there are several artists who have become famous in the racing industry as horse portrait artists. People routinely pay them thousands of dollars to paint portraits of their horses. Several sell their original paintings for tens of thousands of dollars. This woman's work was as good or better than any of those established and successful artists. As a marketing pro, without breaking a sweat, I was able to lay out a plan for her to enter this world, first locally, then nationally, and easily, quickly, make more money in a month than she was currently making all year—and achieve her stated number-one goal in life: to be a stay-at-home mom, there for her kids. Giving such free advice is almost always futile, as it was here. In fact, she had already thought of many of the things I suggested, but had never acted on those thoughts. And she never will.

There are all sorts of reasons for this inaction. Poor self-image, lack of confidence, or not being able to see yourself doing it. Ignorance. Laziness. Procrastination. Waiting for better timing or more resources. The list of excuses for inaction and status quo acceptance is long and, of course, useless and valueless. If you seek to attract wealth into your life, you have to get the list out of your life.

I have had exactly this same experience thousands of times. When I was doing interviews, appearances, and seminars for *How to Make Millions with Your Ideas,* I had almost identical conversations with one person after another. Whenever someone finds out what I do, they tell me of their great idea they've never acted on. Every cab and limo driver has a book he hasn't written and never will. One did, and it led to the HBO series *Taxicab Confessions.* I once spoke at a very special, high-priced seminar for entrepreneurs; experts in direct marketing via home shopping channels like QVC and HSN, infomercials, and radio all spoke and worked with about 100 attendees. Everyone there had an "idea" for a product that would be terrific for sale on QVC. None acted on these ideas, except one, my friend Jeff Paul, who subsequently successfully sold millions of dollars of his invented item on QVC.

Everybody has ideas. Everybody has latent talents. Everybody has ability.

Few act on them.

And make no mistake: there is no wealth to be found *in* an idea. There is only wealth to be had from acting *on* an idea.

This is so important that I want to relate several stories of people I work with to illustrate the way they behave when presented with a worthy idea. The details of their businesses are not all that important, and you should avoid being distracted by them. Instead, focus on the way they responded to ideas and opportunities.

Dr. Paul Searby, a dentist, was experimenting with different possibilities for becoming a consultant in the dental field when he first met with me. In discussing his business, I discovered he had been running a little school for people to become dental assistants, in his dental office on Saturdays, and it made over $150,000.00 a year as a side business. It was so profitable, someone was offering to buy it from him for about $300,000.00. I told him he should put that into a package and sell it to other dentists, one in each market, nationwide. I said it was a huge opportunity, far greater than the several he'd been working on and had come to get my advice on. I told him to shelve everything else and work on this. In less than 30 days, he had his first direct-mail and advertising to interest dentists in this opportunity out the door;

in only a few more weeks, he was giving his first seminar presenting the opportunity and immediately sold several school setup packages at $20,000.00 each. Only a year later, the price is $40,000.00. He has sold nearly 100 schools, sells one to several every week, has sold his dental practice, has financial independence, and works one day a week on this business. Now, this is very important: when he launched his first ads and mailings, filled his first seminar, and began selling schools, he wasn't "ready." The videos of the classes weren't yet taped or edited. Everything he would need to give the dentists wasn't done. He hadn't planned the seminar itself. But he got started. He didn't wait until all his ducks were neatly lined up in a row. As a side effect of his success with this business, Paul has attracted and acted on several other, related opportunities and been invited by leading experts in dentistry to speak at their conferences, write for their newsletters, and do business with their customers.

Bill Glazer owned two clothing stores in Baltimore, which he'd made fabulously successful with unusual and innovative marketing strategies based in large part on ideas he got from my books and courses. He sought me out when he saw I was coming to Baltimore, and we had lunch. When he showed me what he was doing, I told him he should resell all his advertising and marketing to other clothing store owners, and I gave him a business plan to do so. It is a relatively formulaic approach to what I call the "niche information marketing business." Bill immediately began selling his "system" to other clothing store owners, then sporting goods retailers, then jewelers, then furniture store owners, and built a multimillion dollar publishing business. Recently, he bought one of my publishing, coaching, and seminar businesses, now Glazer-Kennedy Inner Circle, which publishes my

No B.S. Marketing Letter, has a monthly teleseminar series, and hosts two large conferences a year. He makes millions of dollars a year as an information marketer and entrepreneur. As a side effect, shortly after Bill began marketing his own information products for retailers, consulting clients began appearing, unasked for, and unsolicited invitations to exchange only his know-how for equity in good businesses poured in, unasked for, unsolicited. Although he has turned most away, the several he has accepted have each proved extremely lucrative. Ultimately, I took the opportunity of selling my main publishing company to him as well.

For years, I have urged all my Members and clients to hire and use celebrities in their marketing. I have undoubtedly told thousands of local business owners of every stripe that they should do this and how to do it. Of those thousands, only two have. The most notable is Scott Tucker, a Chicago mortgage broker. Immediately upon being given this advice in a coaching meeting, he began his search and quickly secured Refrigerator Perry, a legendary Chicago Bear, as his business' celebrity spokesperson. His effective use of The Frig has increased response to his advertising, making every ad dollar produce more, thus increasing the profit margins in his business. It has increased referrals, increased his income, and been helpful in establishing a second business, coaching other mortgage brokers, which was worth more than a million dollars in its first year. Scott didn't do anything at least 300 or 400 other business owners I've given exactly the same advice to couldn't have done— although they haven't.

Some years ago, a professional speaker named Foster Hibbard saw me speak and sell about $50,000.00 of my book/

audio packages from the platform. He sought me out and confessed that, although he was popular, busy, and well-known, in 30 years he'd only earned a modest living from speaking and had never created significant wealth, principally because he worked only for fees and was woefully unsuccessful at selling his audio programs, let alone developing additional income from audience members converted to customers. I have had similar conversations with at least 100 other speakers. In most cases, as with Foster, the speakers are capable, talented, dynamic, effective, but unable to convert their ability and work to wealth. I've said the same things to most of them I said to Foster. None but Foster have ever followed through. In Foster's case, in the 24 months following that conversation, he made well over a million dollars from speaking—by his accounting, more than he'd made in the previous decade! Oh, and almost as soon as Foster began implementing the strategies I gave him, other people sought him out; he was offered numerous speaking opportunities he'd previously been denied. Opportunity knocked on his door as never before.

Do not err in focusing on the fact that none of the above examples have anything to do with the specific, particular business you are in. Consider only the behavioral commonality demonstrated in all of them. And take note of the side effect experienced by all of them.

And let me come at this two more ways. Mike Vance, a close associate of Walt Disney's for many years, consultant to top companies, and author of the book *Think Outside the Box*, tells the story of asking a troubled corporate CEO what his biggest, most vexxing problem was. After he described it, Mike asked, "Who's working on it?" The CEO said, "No one." When Mike asked why, the CEO said, "Because it can't be solved." Against that, consider advice from General Norman Schwarzkopf. For three years, I followed General Schwarzkopf on seminar events, heard his speech so many times I memorized it without trying, and spent a lot of time in backstage "green rooms" talking with him. One of the things that sticks in my mind is his contention that a bad decision or wrong decision is better than no decision because if the decision leads to action, it is easier to correct the course of someone or something already in motion than it is to get someone or something into motion from inertia. In his groundbreaking work *Psycho-Cybernetics,* Dr. Maxwell Maltz presents "zig zagging" and "course correction" as the entire basis for human achievement. He points out that hardly anybody gets to any goal via a straight line, but gets there instead by moving, bumping up against something, moving a different way, bumping, zigging, zagging, but moving, moving, moving.

Finally, let me reveal one of my own, personal "secrets of success." It is a daily discipline I have adhered to for more than 30 years. I'd wager I've neglected it less than 30 days out of the 30 years. I've adhered to it 10,920 out of 10,950 days. Every day, no matter what else I am doing or must do that day, even if in a full day of consulting, traveling across country, or on vacation, I still do one thing, if only one thing, one thing intended to "prime my pump" to create future business for myself or my companies. It may be a small thing: tearing out a magazine article that should interest one of my clients, scrawling a note on it and mailing it. It may be answering one item of correspondence, getting one fax sent, identifying a new, potentially useful contact, jotting a note, or sending a book. But no day passes without me doing at least one such thing. Although it is no longer required, it has been especially important to me over the years because a lot of my income is derived from delivery of services, such as speaking, consulting, coaching, and advertising copywriting; so, in a way, I must sell "it" and make "it." Most professionals stop selling while they're delivering, so they have dry spells, roller coaster ups and downs. I have had more demand than supply of me and waiting lists of clients for many years because of my daily discipline of doing at least one proactive thing to attract business every single day.

"Incredible things happen independently of those you personally create. I call these serendipitous blessings. When you're pushing hard on Door A, someone or something opens Door B. Often, when you look through Door B, what's behind it is much better than what you were going after in the first place. However, you wouldn't have seen Door B open if you hadn't been in the hall pushing on Door A."

— JACK M. ZUFFELT,

AUTHOR OF *THE DNA OF SUCCESS*,

WWW.DNAOFSUCCESS.COM

Wealth Magnet 11
Follow-Up

A lot of people start but few follow through.

My experience with entrepreneurs constantly enjoying a massive and steady flow of customers or clients, with opportunities and wealth streaming to them, is that they think in terms of "process" rather than "incident," and "opportunity" rather than "outcome." And I teach entrepreneurs to think in these terms.

To use myself as example, consider something very simple. As a result of some publicity and promotion for one of the earlier books in the No B.S. Series (*No B.S. Time Management for Entrepreneurs*), I was invited to be interviewed on the syndicated

Chamber of Commerce radio program. Most authors would view this and treat this as an "outcome." Do it. Did it. Over. Done. I view it as "opportunity" because I have and will have other books to promote and have clients with things to promote. So I want this to turn into a continuing relationship rather than a one-night stand, and I know better than to think that occurs by accident. Most authors will hope they'll get invited back, but hope is not a strategy. So immediately after that interview, I sent a nice, personal letter and a gift box with other books and my bobblehead. I got a thank-you letter back. I reply, and gift the hosts with a subscription to my newsletter. Now they get something from me every month. I continue to nurture this relationship. It is, to me, an asset. An asset from which I will draw dividends many times.

A confession: I don't do this as well or as often as I know I should. As excuse, I have my hectic schedule and my anathema to staff. But still, my observation is that I do a lot more of it and do it better than just about anybody else.

My friend Steve Miller, the world class expert in the trade show industry, and my Gold/VIP Member Mitch Carson of Impact Products, a consultant as well as a supplier of exhibits, promotional merchandise, and marketing tools to trade show exhibitors, will both tell you that 90% of all the leads generated by exhibitors spending fortunes at trade shows are NEVER followed up. This matches my own experience when attending trade shows and asking for information, inviting follow-up. Unfortunately, exhibitors and the sales professionals working for them view the act of exhibiting as an "outcome" more than as an "opportunity." Consequently, the vast majority of exhibitors are constantly unhappy with the return on investment from exhibiting!

Bring it all the way down to the simplest of situations. Your own daily life. When you dine at a restaurant for the first time, get clothes cleaned at a dry cleaners for the first time, and go into a different shop of one kind or another for the first time. Of the many, many times you do this, how many times have you immediately gotten a follow-up letter from the restaurant or shop owner thanking you for coming in and inviting you back? How many have sent you an interesting newsletter every month afterward, to create and maintain a presence with you?* The answer will be: hardly any. Or none. Your entering and departing their place of business is an "outcome" to them. To me, the person coming in for the very first time is a magnificent "opportunity." The way you view it will determine what you do about it. Few businesses have any set means of identifying first-time customers, of getting their contact information to follow-up. Even fewer do follow-up. But I assure you, those few who do prosper as a result.

Now let's talk about "process" versus "incident." For many years, a big part of my income—and wealth creation via acquisition of customers—came from speaking. I've also coached, consulted, and trained over 1,000 other professional speakers, and I have closely observed the behavior of speakers. Most, when they get a booking, put a gold star on its date on the calendar. Later they go there, speak, get paid, and that's it. For them, it's an "incident." When I got a booking, I put the gold star on its date, then devised and implemented a complex, multistep, multimedia "attack" to boost the client's attendance at his event, to motivate those coming to be eager to hear me and be in the room, and to precondition the audience to be responsive to me so I could sell more from the stage. I had a similar plan for after the speech, to spread my tentacles in the client's company and get more speaking, consulting, and other opportunities, and to follow-up on those in attendance as well as those not in attendance who did not buy what I offered to sell to them after the fact. I viewed the speaking engagement as only one part of a "process."

To take this to a more "ordinary" business, consider the quick oil change shop in your neighborhood. They probably have a process in place to do upsells—additional things you need, like a new oil filter. They probably capture your contact information and send you a reminder postcard when it's about time for your next oil change. But that's it, and there's so much more they could do. For example, they could try to sell you a coupon book of prepaid services at a discount. They could find out about your spouse's car or other cars in your family. They could immediately identify your neighbors via the criss-cross directory and send them a letter with coupons noting you were a happy customer. They could be crosspromoting with a car wash. They should put you on their newsletter list so they "visit" you every month. They should get your birthday and send you a card. Rather than viewing your coming in for an oil change as an "incident," they should view it as the start of a multifaceted, continuing "process."

This requires a shift in the way you view your customers and prospects—as people to randomly sell something to or as your most valuable assets to build and maintain a solid fence around, to care for, coddle, and develop a strong relationship with, and to multiply through referrals.

*You can have a monthly newsletter done for you! There is a *Good News Letter* for consumers, and a *Good Business News Letter* for business owners, featuring articles by me! You can obtain it every month on diskette to drop in your offer of the month and identity and use as you see fit, or have the entire project done for you: newsletter customized, your list maintained, and your newsletter printed and mailed for you. For information, go online to www.petetheprinter.com or fax a request to (330) 922-9833.

Wealth Magnet 12
Integrity

Relax. I'm not about to deliver a morality lecture. In fact, we can forget all about the very idea of morality for this discussion. We can simply be pragmatic.

Pragmatism basically means doing what best serves your interests. Doing what delivers the results you desire. Doing what works.

You need not think in terms of doing what's right at all.

Let's just talk about doing the right things as pragmatists. Not what's right morally. What's right pragmatically.

The number-one complaint everybody has about the people and companies they do business with, buy from, get mad at, and stop buying from is that the vendor doesn't keep his promises.

In my private coaching groups, I currently have four lawyers. Out of 63 people, 4 are lawyers. It's not by design! I try to discourage them, but there they are. And they've confirmed for me as fact: the number-one reason lawyers lose clients AND the number-one cause of complaints against lawyers to bar associations is not incompetence or malpractice, not overcharging, not failure—it is merely and simply not communicating with clients. In the printing industry, where I've owned businesses, have clients, done a lot of work, and spent millions myself, the number-one reason that clients fire printers and go elsewhere is missed deadlines. In the restaurant industry, the number-one reason that companies stop ordering for delivery from a particular restaurant is late delivery.

> In virtually every business, the number-one factor in losing customers and turning customers into bad news spreaders is actually very, very simple. It can be summarized as "stated or implicit promises not kept."

Conversely, one of the biggest Wealth Attractants ever invented is simply saying what you will do and doing what you say. When you become known for absolute reliability, customers, clients, opportunity, and money will flow to you in ever increasing abundance. The word spreads because you are so rare. Price competition becomes irrelevant.

Like everyone else, I occasionally get myself into a situation where I can't meet a deadline, can't keep a promise. I am maniacal about every commitment, from simple punctuality to the more complex seriously, so the operable word is "occasionally." It makes me nuts when this happens because, as a pragmatist, I know how detrimental to my interests it is. When it does occur, I've learned not to run and hide or ignore it and hope it goes unnoticed, but to confront it, apologize, and make it right. Again, not out of ethical or moral obligation but out of pragmatism. I'm choosing the best business strategy.

And here's something rather "advanced" that very few entrepreneurs ever discover: a less appealing promise kept serves you better than making a more appealing promise you can't, won't, or don't keep.

Wealth Magnet 13
Ask

This is even Biblical. *Ask and ye shall receive.*

And everybody knows it. You don't ask; you don't get. Yet a whole lot of people who know it don't actually practice it much. They go through life wanting all sorts of things they never seem to work up the courage to ask for. So they're unhappy in their businesses because they don't ask their clients, vendors and employees. They're unhappy in their marriages because they don't ask their spouses. By "ask," I mean a composite of things. Clearly enunciating your desires, expectations, and, when appropriate, demands. Asking people to do things as you want them done. Seeking co-operation and support.

Even fewer people ask "outsiders."

I've found that it's perfectly okay to ask for a lot from a lot of people. I ask people for information, advice, ideas, contacts and introductions, and all sorts of assistance, pretty much with impunity. I am also generous with reciprocity and reward. But I ask.

> ### "I Want It All.
> ### And I Want It Delivered."
>
> —MAGNET ON MY REFRIGERATOR

Just for example, I had over 250 different people involved in the initial promotion for the book you are reading and the other books in the No B.S. series. I got this publisher to do things they have not done for any other author (which they'd prefer I didn't mention). I got famous and not-so-famous authors and speakers to send e-mails to their lists, "plug" the books in their speeches and newsletters, and put information about the books up on their web sites. I got over 2.5 million (!) e-mails sent for me at zero cost. I got people to pay to host promotional events and tele-seminars. On and on and on. Mostly because I asked. Did I get everybody I asked to participate? No. But I got a whole lot more people to participate than if I hadn't asked everybody. Did I get everybody to do everything I wanted them to do? No. But I got a lot more than if I hadn't asked.

I know a few other authors who are great askers. My friend, Mark Victor Hansen, co-creator with Jack Canfield of the publishing phenomenon, the *Chicken Soup for the Soul* series, is a phenomenal asker. If he meets a celebrity, king, president, athlete, CEO, anybody and everybody, he asks them for something, to somehow help him promote himself or his books or his causes, to introduce him to somebody else he wants to meet. You might think such asking, asking, asking would repel people and wind up with you standing alone as if you had body odor, but the opposite occurs. The asking is magnetic. Actually, people, especially successful people, like being asked for their ideas, opinions, and advice, like being asked for their help and influence. Often, you even get more than you ask for! There's another author who called up Trump's office "cold" and asked to have The Donald look at his book manuscript and give him a quote. Trump gave him a quote and an entire extra chapter to add to the book, a lot of marketing muscle for the book.

With that in mind, I'd like to ask YOU to promote this book. Go to www.nobsbooks.com, and click on "viral." There, you'll find some ready-to-use e-mails you can forward, free articles you can copy and send, and all sorts of nifty goodies you can give to your entrepreneur friends. And if you happen to be an association executive, corporate big dog, or somebody else with a big list of businesspeople who know you and respect you, I'd be happy to hear from you personally, and we can figure out something—maybe a special free teleseminar you gift to everybody, for example. I'm game. Send me a fax with some details at (602) 269-3113. (Please be patient. It might be two to three weeks before I can respond.)

See, I asked.

Of course, there is something of a science to asking effectively, too complex to discuss here. And it helps to be able to give to get, or least reciprocate to get. It's not essential, but it is helpful. If you're really, really perceptive you'll realize how I've used this book, done things within this book, to support my asking for assistance promoting the book. If you figure it out, it's a secret not limited to authors and books. Any business owner could use the same strategy.

Wealth Magnet 14
Domino Opportunity

A lot of entrepreneurs get gifted with a lot of opportunity. It's not just lack or shortage of opportunity that explains anybody's lack of wealth.

Phil McGraw was a family therapist who disliked private practice, dabbled in speaking, the personal growth seminar business, corporate consulting on human resources matters, and even consulting with lawyers on jury selection and witness preparation. He was handed the gift of consulting with the lawyers hired to defend Oprah Winfrey when she was sued over her negative remarks about beef. Lots of consultants would have collected a fat fee and an autographed photo and been happy to get them, and that would be that. Dr. Phil became Dr. Phil by dominoing that opportunity.

You may never get such a giant and obvious opportunity. But you most certainly do get many opportunities, day in, day out, that you fail to domino.

As a personal example, a trade journal for attorneys, *Pennsylvania Lawyer,* published a chapter from my *No B.S. Time Management* book as an article. I immediately went into the domino-the-opportunity mode. A copy of the article and book was sent to the other 49 states' law journals to try and get published, to promote my books, in those magazines. A copy of the article went to several clients who market to lawyers, run seminars for lawyers, etc., with encouragement to reprint the article and distribute it to their customers. Sure, it's a small thing. But you sell 50,000 books one book at a time. So it's all about small things multiplied, as is most marketing and promotion. So one article dominoed into 5 or 8 or 20 is a small thing multiplied equaling a big thing.

As another example, consider Susan Berkeley, a member of one of my coaching groups and a professional voice coach. Actually, you'd know her voice from AT&T commercials. Susan was brought in to coach competitors on Donald Trump's show *The Apprentice,* during the 2005 season. We knew about 90 days ahead of time that the episode involving her coaching would air. We didn't know for sure if she would appear in the episode. And she was sworn to secrecy prior to the episode's airing, so no advance promotion was possible. But it was and is a fact that she coached the competing apprentices on speaking, voice, and presentation skills. To domino this, Susan obtained the domain name www.apprenticevoicecoach.com. She assembled both a New

York City media list (where she lives) and a national media list, ready to begin firing e-mails, faxs, FedExs, and phone calls at 10:01 P.M. the night the episode aired, making her available the next morning for interviews and commentary on who won and who lost and why. In total, she and I devised and organized over 20 different advertising, marketing, publicity, and promotion strategies, campaigns, and initiatives to occur starting the morning after and to continue for three months after the episode's airing. As I'm finishing this book before all this occurs, I can't tell you of any of the results, although you may find further discussion of this in the free e-mail course tied to this book, which you can obtain at www.nobsbooks.com. But the important point is, Susan will do everything she or I can conceive of to domino this single, in actuality, tiny opportunity.

Wealth Magnet 15
Passion

There's a whole lot of metaphysical foolishness in books, tapes, and seminars pushing the simplistic premise: do what you love to do and money will follow. Now there is a giant, steaming, stinking pile of b.s.! Sure, happy accidents happen, but do you want to wager your future on freak incidents?

I like to lie in a hammock. I like to read. Eat pizza. Watch football. I have yet to figure out how to get people to line up and pay to watch me do that. Doesn't matter how much I enjoy those things. My enjoyment can multiply; the money won't.

This idea that you can do what you like or feel most passionately about and be assured of attracting wealth is silly and childish. Appealing, certainly. But silly and childish.

Wealth comes through businesses, and businesses must be market driven, *not* personal joy driven. Market driven. The list of people who got out of bed this morning hoping you will have passion and joy today is probably short. But the lists of people who get out of bed in the morning with diseases they desperately want cures for, problems they urgently seek solutions for, hopes and dreams they need help fulfilling, and conveniences they'd welcome if offered, those lists are long. If you want to attract maximum wealth with minimum effort in minimum time, here's the formula: find such a list that you can "engineer" your own superior answer for.

You *do* want to avoid drudgery. No one can maintain self-motivation and productivity for very long while engaged in activities they find mind-numbing or onerous, or dealing with people they despise, or doing work they find unfulfilling, or selling things they do not believe in. This is a certain path to poverty. But, on the other hand, only doing what you like with no regard to market demand is nearly as certain a path to poverty.

Truth is, you rarely get all the results you want only from activities and processes you prefer. Maturity involves opting for desirable results rather than pleasing activities.

There's also a popular metaphysical idea—don't pursue money, pursue passion. Pfui. I'm a writer, and I like Mark Twain's quote, "No one but a blockhead writes but for money." I hear people say they like their work so much they'd do it even if they weren't being paid. I think that's frightening and dangerous. Someone in business needs to think in a businesslike way. Why would I write just to write? I write for an audience who will pay money. Otherwise, it's like being the tree that falls in the distant, unpopulated forest, heard or noticed by no one. What's the point?

So, let's try rearranging some items. In no particular order:

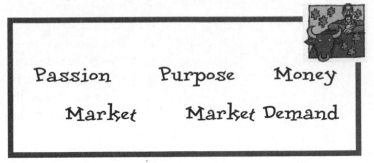

Passion   Purpose   Money

Market   Market Demand

The very unbusinesslike arrangement would be: passion, purpose, market, market demand, money. Pursue your passion, indulge your purpose or mission, with no regard for a market or market demand, and hope to attract wealth. I again say to you that hope is not a strategy.

The business arrangement would be: market, market demand, purpose, passion, money. Identify a viable, preferably underserved market, determine market demand (what it wants most and will pay for), then align your purpose, and do something for the market that you can feel passionately about.

Wealth Magnet 16
See What Isn't There

I n 1982, I started a company from scratch with less than $1,000.00 that produced millions of dollars over the next several years and produced customers that continue contributing to my income today. It was classic entrepreneurial alchemy—nothing but an idea on a Monday and $100,000.00 in income by the following Friday. Before the Internet, incidentally. At the risk of distracting you from the point, I'll give you the specifics but with the warning to focus on the principle.

At the time, in the chiropractic profession information and advice about practice marketing, promotion, and success was being delivered to doctors at two price levels: through very inexpensive books and tapes, $10.00 to $100.00, and in multiyear practice management programs, costing upwards of $25,000.00. There was nothing in between. Further, the way practice management was sold was via small, free introductory seminars, city by city by city. As a result, 30 or 40 doctors in a town would attend, eager for help, but only one might be willing to make the required investment. *The business I created stepped into the gap, the empty market space in the middle.* I followed the practice management companies, again put those 30 or 40 doctors into a seminar, but offered them a $300.00 to $500.00 alternative. Virtually 100% bought. In 36 months, more than 10,000 of only 35,000 chiropractors in the entire profession bought one or more of our courses—an amazing 30% market share. Now, forget all about chiropractors and seminars and courses. Focus on stepping into the empty or underserved market space.

At the time a client of mine created Steak 'n Ale restaurants, there were a lot of "premium" steakhouses, like Ruth Chris' and Morton's, and a lot of very low-end steakhouses, like Sizzler, but hardly anything in between. He developed a restaurant that combined the ambiance, the "feel," and the quality of a premium steakhouse with pricing in between the two extremes. And he got very rich.

For years, air travel options were fly commercial, coach or first class, charter a private plane, or own your own jet. A few companies, notably including NetJets, in which Warren Buffet invested, found market space in the middle. Bringing the time sharing and fractional ownership formats from real estate, they created fractional jet ownership. Many celebrities as well as CEOs, executives, and entrepreneurs are "owners"/clients of these companies. Famous names you know like Martha Stewart own as well as lots of people you don't know. And these companies were well positioned to benefit from the 9/11 tragedy. Immediately after 9/11, these companies were flooded with new buyers, people who were unwilling to suffer the suddenly heightened inconvenience and time loss of ordinary commercial air travel. (One man's tragedy is always another's opportunity.)

The unused market space is not always in the middle, but there is often space between extremes of price or location. Sometimes, the space is at the top. My client Dr. Charles Martin is a top cosmetic dentist with a Taj Mahal spa-style office featuring a wide array of patient comforts, from paraffin hand waxes and massage to lattes and fresh-baked cookies. His average case's fee is 200% to 500% higher than that of his nearby, competing dentists. Sometimes the space is at the bottom—although I generally dislike this place. Still, Wal-Mart is, of course, the ultimate example of the moment, of grabbing empty space both at the bottom of the price ladder and, initially, in locations other chains ignored. Sometimes, it's in a means of distribution. My friend the late E. Joseph Cossman, a mail-order guru, made ten different million-dollar businesses out of products sold by their manufacturers through only one or two means of distribution. He secured exclusive rights to the ignored distribution channels. My friend Joe Sugarman took sunglasses to TV infomercials, then QVC. Omaha Steaks is simply steaks sold by mail-order, delivered by UPS.

Cosmetics, skin care products, and acne treatment products have long been at a number of different price points, from discount to outrageous, via department store cosmetic counters, free-standing stores, mall kiosks, catalogs, and direct sales and network marketing organizations like Avon, Amway, or Mary

Kay. Guthy-Renker, my long-time client, has virtually dominated distribution through TV infomercials for a decade, with its Victoria Principal, Connie Selleca, Susan Lucci, and other celebrity lines, and the Pro-Activ acne treatment products developed at my urging.

Looking for the ideal gap for you to fill is a very nuts and bolts piece of advice, possibly more appropriate for one of my marketing books than this book. But I include it here for a broader purpose, as an illustration of the kind of thinking that attracts wealth. The cliché is "think outside the box." But I suppose it is a cliché because it is so laden with truth. Even savvy, clever, aggressive entrepreneurs fall into inside-the-box thinking. It's easy and dangerous to see our opportunities only in terms of incremental improvements of what we already do and the way we do it, essentially pushing at the sides of the box. I take pride in the fact that clients who come to me for consulting days, are in coaching groups, or attend my yearly Renegade Millionaire Retreat* frequently say the same thing, "I came to Kennedy thinking I was in one business; I left in an entirely different, infinitely better, and more valuable business."

*Information about my Renegade Millionaire Retreats, Renegade Millionaire System and *Renegade Millionaire* magazine is online at www.renegademillionairesystem.com

The challenge is to see what is not there. As an example, consider this statement by the CEO of Home Depot, made in an interview in 2005:

> *Experts say we are in a $400 billion market, because that's the market for our products TODAY. But I say we are in a $900 billion market. We're focusing on selling differently to professional contractors and that's a $300 billion market itself. The "we-do-it-for-you" market is another $200 billion market itself.*

In 2003–2004, this company experienced a 26% increase in sales of home installation and do-it-for-them services to what they call the "free spending, do-it-for-me-now consumer."

Of course, if you carefully analyze all this, there's trading of dollars from one category to another, so adding each on top of the other is delusional. There are assumptions worthy of question. Still, the main point is the vision, the ability of this CEO to see what is not yet there, to see gaps and opportunities, empty or underserved market space. In the February 17, 2005, issue of *USA Today*, there was an article in the Science Section headlined "A WHOLE NEW WAY OF LOOKING AT THE WORLD."

Bill Glazer used it as fodder for a sales letter about my Renegade Millionaire Retreat, saying "More important to me than just the millions of dollars I've made going in the directions Dan has pointed me, is that, quite literally, Dan has shown me a whole new way of looking at the world."

He went on to write, "There are hundreds and hundreds of people who were in 'small businesses' who are now super-entrepreneurs with multiple streams of income they never imagined, with clientele they never conceived, charging prices or fees they never thought possible, being sought out rather than having to chase business."

I have the newspaper clipping up on my bulletin board as my own reminder of the mandate to keep looking at the world, at my world and at my clients' worlds in a whole new way—frequently.

How can you keep your thoughts about your own opportunities flexible, agile, and outside rather than inside the box? The most important key is exposure to a lot of ideas, information, news, business success stories, and people outside the box of your business and your industry. I wrote another book in the No B.S. series just for this reason: *No B.S. Direct Marketing for NON-Direct Marketing Businesses.* You need to read, or at least skim, not just your trade journals, but also others' trade journals. Read good, well-researched, cutting-edge newsletters (like mine!). You need a lot of ideas, examples, and information flowing to you from diverse sources. Most entrepreneurs seem to operate as if they were Amish, locked away in a closed society.

I encourage people to be in coaching groups and mastermind groups, ours or others. You need association, in person, or via teleconference with forward-thinking, forward-looking, flexible, innovative, and successful entrepreneurs. In my groups, as of this writing, we have a person who owns a house painting company, who in several years in the groups, has added a deck refinishing and handyman service. There's the owner of a promotional products company, who, in several years, has grown his company by acquisition and added a whole new business as well. There are also several lawyers, a dentist, an inventor and manufacturer, a martial arts school owner and franchiser, a professional voice coach, several from the real estate industry, a chiropractor, a college planning advisor, and a number of consultants to different industries. Most came with one inside the box business. They've used imagination, evolution, and revolution to develop multiple synergistic businesses. They have benefited enormously from each others' ideas, pointed and challenging questioning, and encouragement. The commonalities are only income and wealth, philosophy, and use of smart direct marketing strategies. This is the kind of support environment you need to get into or create for yourself. It's very, very hard to attract wealth working in a vacuum.

Wealth Magnet 17
No Boundaries

I f you are my age, 50+, or even 40+, or maybe even 30+, you are very likely to think provincially. You will have a preference for doing business with vendors within easy driving distance. If you own a local business, you will think mostly about local marketing to local customers. If you are under the age of 35, you will have grown up with the internet and that alone will have given you a very different viewpoint. Because I gravitated to what was then called "mail-order" and never had a bricks-'n-mortar business, I never thought locally. On the other hand, because of my age, it's still more natural for me to think provincially rather than globally.

There are no geographic boundaries for wealth attraction. And most businesses can and should be enlarged and expanded to national or international scope. That's easy to understand in businesses like mine: information businesses. I can deliver a newsletter anywhere. The internet has accelerated and eased the global spreading of my persona and messages. While I always had a small number of subscribers and Members overseas, today revenues from outside the United States are approaching 30% of my business. But *everybody* should get beyond local or regional to national or international. Let me give you a few examples.

Darin Garman was a real estate broker specializing in apartment buildings and commercial properties in Iowa. Naturally, most of his buyers and investors were also in Iowa. He was enormously successful, so he controlled over 70% of all such transactions in his primary geographic market, Cedar Rapids and neighboring communities. At my urging, he began advertising nationally in publications like *Forbes* and *Investors Business Daily* to interest investors all over America in the conservative "heartland of America" real estate investments. Today, over half of all his sales of Iowa properties are to investors in New York, California, and almost every other state, mostly sight unseen, never even meeting the investors in person. There are many benefits of bringing these investors in from all over America rather than just seeking them locally. For example, they are less price sensitive, not biased by what they "know" as area residents; they are making their decisions purely based on the mathematical merits of the investment. Also, although there is obviously a limited, finite number of wealthy individuals interested in owning apartment buildings in Cedar Rapids, there's a virtually unlimited, infinite number of such wealthy individuals spread out all over

America. Next, at my urging, Darin is reaching out to investors overseas. Also, he and I have worked together to develop an unusual kind of investing device or format, a certain type of fund, that enables investors to enter with smaller sums and/or to spread their risk over a wide variety of properties, with guaranteed minimum annual returns; with this investment, the reach is global.

Matt Furey, like me, is an author. His first book on fitness, still a bestseller (although never on a bestseller list) is, *Combat Conditioning*. For a long time, the only means for an author to attempt converting his knowledge and intellectual property to wealth was through bookstores, a very limited means of distribution, provincial multiplied. Matt chose to ignore the traditional publishing industry entirely and has sold hundreds of thousands of copies entirely via his own direct-response ads in magazines and his web sites. But for Matt, the book is just the beginning. If you visit mattfurey.com, you'll enter a complex web of web sites, e-mail newsletters, and other online marketing generating millions of dollars a year. Matt spends two months a year on combination vacation and research trips in China, spends an enormous amount of time with his family, and works as he wishes. I've consulted with and coached Matt in the early stages of his business, and most recently sold one of my publishing companies to him (The Psycho-Cybernetics Foundation, www.psycho-cybernetics.com). His mastery of the internet makes a person in an isolated town in Afghanistan, a U.S. soldier on a base in a foreign land, or a young man "with sand kicked in his face" in Africa just as viable a customer as someone working out at a local gym. But Matt is not alone, nor is the globally expansive power of the internet limited to books, tapes, and other information products.

Think of entire industries liberated from local or locale-to-locale boundaries by direct marketing: mail-order, toll free numbers, the internet. It wasn't all that long ago that the only way you could buy or sell stocks was through your local broker at his local office. Antiques were sold in antique shops, art in galleries, not on eBay or web sites. I could fill the remainder of the book with examples.

Even the reach of the professional practice has gone from a five-mile radius to the world. You only need to skim the pages of any airline's magazine stuffed in the seat pockets, and you'll find full-page advertisements from cosmetic dentists, doctors treating carpel tunnel syndrome, and doctors treating menopause. They advertise nationally, attracting patients who fly to them from all over the country. Why would someone who lives in Illinois go to a dentist in Houston, Texas? If you read this entire book carefully, you will understand the market forces and Wealth Attraction Magnets that make this happen. Incidentally, I live in Ohio, but my dentist is in Richmond, Virginia, and my personal physician who assists with my management of my diabetes (without prescription drugs) is in San Antonio, Texas.

When you transcend geographic boundaries, you instantly and automatically increase your wealth attraction power and opportunities.

Wealth Magnet 18
Clarity

I t's *instructive to ask business owners how much money they* expect to receive today, tomorrow, next week.

Most are playing blind archery. Few have clear, definite expectations. This is grievous negligence as expectations have a great deal to do with results. It's also dereliction of managerial duty. It is up to you to decide—key word: *decide*—how much money you will receive today, this week, this month, this year, in advance, based upon your marketing and management plans, your prescheduled actions and initiatives. If you board an airplane and ask the pilot, "Where are we going today? When are we scheduled to get there?" and he's not sure, exit immediately!

For the pilot of a business, today's destination and arrival time is measured in dollars going into the bank account, customers captured for development, and a few other key pieces of data. If you're not sure about those things, the odds of arriving at the right destination by happy accident aren't good.

Ask a restaurant owner: "How much business are you going to do today?" He'll answer, "I don't know. It depends on who comes in." That's a lousy answer.

If you're running a restaurant, you have to have a very good idea of how many are coming in, if not who's coming in. You have a number of customers who've bought membership cards so you're dinging their credit cards the first of each month and sending them five coupons. You've sent a certain number of birthday cards out with coupons the week before. You've faxed the week's specials to your business lunch customers, and you have certain expectations based on all this activity.

This gets us to the big topic of clarity. Clarity about what you don't want, what you do want, the income you expect, the net worth increases you expect, and the reasons for your expectations. I have long operated my businesses by numbers, knowing what the minimum amount my time must be worth, what a project must produce, and what sales will come from an appearance in front of an audience. I track day by day whether or not I am "on schedule" to hit my income and wealth targets for the week, month, quarter, year. If you don't know whether or not you are on schedule, it's a safe bet you aren't. If you're assessing how well you're doing with your goals for the year in October, it's too late. You need to assess how well you are doing at noon on January 2nd—and January 3rd, 4th, and 5th.

I have clear, vivid mental pictures of what my business, business life, and life are to look like. I have detailed, constantly up-dated plans to support the pictures. I'm very clear about intentions and expectations. Sure, there's the axiom: if you want to hear God laugh, tell him your plans; and sure, things go awry. Also, fortunately, unexpected, better opportunities present themselves. But imperfect results from clarity are still far superior to random results. Clarity sets up magnetized targets you are drawn to. It allows your conscious and subconscious minds to work in tandem.

I'm also very clear about my schedule and work days. They aren't just planned, they are scripted. And well over 80% unfold exactly as scripted, producing exactly the results intended and expected. If this interests you, read *No B.S. Time Management for Entrepreneurs.*

Wealth is attracted to clarity. Paul J. Meyer, founder of Success Motivation Institute, a former insurance salesman who turned himself into a very wealthy entrepreneur with a number of business interests and extensive real estate investments, and an author on success subjects said, "If you are not achieving your goals, it is probably because they are not clearly defined." It's not that the individual lacks essential skills, opportunities, or resources to achieve his goals; it is a problem with the goals themselves.

I personally have found times that I wander astray from productivity and profit, and was not seeing the money stream come in as it usually does for me; I've gotten foggy about my own intentions and objectives or negligent about measurement of progress.

Wealth Magnet 19
Independence

Wealth is attracted to wealth, money to money. But because independence is the prime outcome and benefit of wealth, wealth is also attracted to independence. One is as good as the other as a magnet.

Consequently, *the less you need income, the more opportunities present themselves, the more eager people are to do business with you and pay you money, and the more easily wealth is attracted.* This mandates the simple practice of living beneath your present income so that you can be and stay debt free.

There are major differences of opinion about this, but this is my book, so I will give you my opinion, based on what has worked so very well for me. I realize this is very conservative financial advice. But from my perspective, it is not just financial advice. It is directed at your inner being, subconscious mind, confidence, and at your outer behavior. It is, again, about attracting wealth more than it is part of a debate about using debt as investment capital. That debate ignores the psychology of attracting wealth.

Dave Ramsey, a popular radio host I like and respect, who deals with money topics, agrees with me about getting and staying debt free for practical purposes. Many other financial gurus differ passionately. They would advise, for example, fully mortgaging your home in periods of low interest rates and investing that money in real estate, stocks, or whatever to make the spread and build up assets. I have never gotten comfortable with debt as an asset, with leveraging debt into more debt. I also have a much longer view of history than most seem to have. I remember, for example, the Jimmy Carter years and the Houston real estate crash when people so leveraged were wiped out en masse. I also find that leverage-the-debt advice often comes from people who earn commissions selling investments. However, right now, this is not about that debate. The debate ignores and omits the psychology of attracting wealth by feeling wealthy at your core (not indebted) and by feeling and being independent.

Debt doesn't just enslave through compound interest reversed. It enslaves by imposition, by telling you that you should do work you don't want to do, accept clients or customers you can't stand, and otherwise compromise every which way because you need money. I insist your objective should be to get to the position of not needing more income, so you can act independently, be selective, call your own shots, and be entirely free of actual or felt pressure. What I call "The Independent Position" rolls finances, attitude, reality and emotions, and the conscious and subconscious together, and it is magic.

DEBT IS EVIL because . . .

- Every dollar you bring in is *instantly diminished* in value by its need to contribute to servicing your debt.
- It *compels* you to do things you would otherwise not do. Debt produces need. Need is completely counter-productive.
- It leaves you *vulnerable* to short-term competitive or marketplace challenges, economic slumps, aberrant events (e.g., 9/11), etc. that you might otherwise painlessly withstand.
- It is *habit-forming*. It is easy to get good at juggling debt, comfortable living in debt. You can get so good at survival skills that they are in the way of developing success skills.
- It is a *source of worry*, anxiety, and frustration that interferes with wealth attraction, productivity, and even physical health.
- It *lengthens the time required* to get to your Financial Independence Number, sufficient assets and investments that you never need work or earn another dollar for the rest of your life.

Everybody needs to be cautious of need. After all, if you ask most people why they go to work in the morning, they say, "to pay bills." Very high income people say the same thing. And they are still slaves, just better dressed, because they are working for debt.

Entrepreneurs need to be especially cautious of expanding need by piling on employees, infrastructure, overhead, people, places, and things. Bigger is not necessarily better. More gross may not only produce less net but also may move you from master to slave before you realize it. I once worked briefly as a business owner to meet the payroll, pay the bills, and restock the inventory, getting any scraps that might be left over. I didn't like it. And it put me into a mental state completely antithetical to wealth attraction.

In my Renegade Millionaire System (www.renegademillion aire.com), I devote a large amount of time and energy to defining and extolling the virtues of autonomy. I believe it is THE objective that should govern the setting of all other objectives and that it is a closed loop: the pursuit of autonomy best attracts wealth, which facilitates autonomy.

Whether through debt-reduced or debt-free living, other strategies, psychological techniques, or all of these things, I can assure you that the less you need the next deal, the next sale, the next client, or the next dollar, the easier it will be to attract all the deals, sales, clients, and dollars you could ever desire or imagine, times ten.

Wealth Magnet 20
Think Value, Not Time

P eople in prison "do time." Unless you are reading this book while actually behind bars, you don't want to indulge in this same kind of thinking.

People in prison and criminals are not the only people who try to steal money. Actually, a lot of people who appear to be stand-up citizens go through their entire lives trying to steal money. Many succeed but only to a limited degree. Their theft stands in the way of attracting wealth and abundance. Their theft puts them in a prison of their own making.

People who work in factories, especially if union employees, think years on the job should translate to wage increases. This is why wage earners rarely attract wealth. Their erroneous, greedy thinking is in the way. Although it is corporate CEOs and entrepreneurs who are usually accused by the media or viewed by the public as greedy, it is actually these wage workers who exhibit greed at its worst. They want something for nothing; they seek an unfair exchange. Time on a job, years doing a job, does not increase the inherent value of the job being done. In most cases, after the first few years, it doesn't increase the value of the employee either. He doesn't bring 30 years' experience to the table at all. He only brings one year of experience repeated 30 times.

The entrepreneur dare not fall into this belief system trap, because he is devoid of false protections. He is at full mercy of a marketplace with its own brand of harsh justice, based on real value. Wealth is a reflection of actual value to the world. If you want to attract more wealth, you make yourself more valuable. Your value does not increase just because you hang around for years.

One of my Members, Judith Z. told me of one of her employees who every year comes to her and needs a raise. Because they need it, you are, of course, obligated to give it. That's how they think. *I've hung around for another year, so I'm entitled to more money. I need more money, so I should get it.* This is how they think. You can never think this way. Owning your business for ten years does not entitle you to anything more than your newest competitor of one year. What you get comes from the value you create and deliver.

Let me illustrate how completely devoid of integrity this time-on-the-job thinking is. You own a convenience store and you sell coffee for $1.00 per cup. Every morning, the same customer

Ideas for Increasing Your Personal Value

- *Expertise*—what you know
- *Expert Status*—what you are known to know
- *Skill*—what you do
- *Productivity*—what you get done
- *Efficiency*—how you get done what you get done
- *Effectiveness*—opportunity selection and how well you do what you get done
- *Organization/Multiplication*—how you get things done by means other than manual labor
- *Influence*—what you can get others to do
- *Relationships*—who you know
- *Celebrity Status*—how well you are known (by your target audience)
- *Reputation*—what others know about you
- *Vision*—what you see that others don't

comes in, gets a cup of coffee, and pays his dollar. After a year, he comes in and points a gun at your head. He says, "I've been here every day for a year. That's tenure. I've been exchanging a dollar for a cup of coffee. Solely because I've made that value exchange for a year, I'm now going to take two cups of coffee for the same one dollar. You're going to let me, or I'll shoot you in the head."

> Wealth and value and real integrity are all linked together. Anyone trying to get more wealth without providing more value is dishonest and unethical and immoral, and is attempting to defy the fundamental laws of life.

So the employee comes to Judith Z. every year and needs her annual raise. And every year, Judith sits down with her and says, "Fine, you've got a raise, as soon as you enroll in this course and you go to this seminar and you study these books and recordings. And as soon as you do, your raise is a done deal, but not immediately after you finish. As soon as you do these three things and get started, the raise is a done deal."

My question to her was, "How many years have you gone without giving her a raise?"

Her answer is, "14."

This employee wants more money but is unwilling to do anything to deliver more value.

You must avoid making the same unreasonable demands, the same demands devoid of integrity, of the universe. Instead, if you'd like to attract more wealth, do the opposite. Do something that increases the value you bring to your business, your work, or your clients or customers. Increase your value, and you will attract increased wealth.

Wealth Magnet 21
Think Equity, Not Income

This is big.

Most entrepreneurs wake up every morning thinking about how they can make more sales, get more customers, and increase their incomes. These thoughts are ricocheting around in their heads even as they stumble toward the bathroom or coffeemaker. And most entrepreneurs devote enormous thought, time, and energy to these same issues all day long, all month long, all year long. At the end of each day, they try to assess how the day turned out in terms of income. But very few entrepreneurs give the same thought, time, and energy to increasing "value" and "equity."

Income is temporary and perishable. Value and equity can be built to last. Right now, your daily thoughts, your daily measurements are probably weighted 80%, 90%, even 100% to increasing income, and only 20%, 10% or 0% to increasing value and equity. The right balance is 50%/50%.

How can you possibly manage and measure increases in equity daily, like you can income? Actually, there are a number of ways. One of the best is what I call "Future Banking."

Most business owners are focused on Present Banking. If you ask a restaurant operator how his day was, he might cite number of meals served, number of customers who came in, or sales. But he will not talk about any measured equity increase, what I call "Future Banking," and he will not have given it a thought.

I teach Future Banking in depth in my "Wealth Attraction System" and "Renegade Millionaire System*." Here is a simplified summary. First, income is income and does not necessarily convert to wealth. In fact, income is usually spent. Income increases do not necessarily translate to wealth either. Wealth is wealth. It comes from value and equity. Second, there is Present

*There are SEVEN WAYS TO DEVELOP EQUITY in any business. This subject is discussed in complete detail in the free e-mail course that is a companion to this book. Enroll free at www.nobsbooks.com.

Banking and Future Banking. The really astute entrepreneur works on both simultaneously, not sequentially. He thinks about value, not just income.

We'll use our restaurant owner again as example. My client and Platinum Member Rory Fatt, president of Restaurant Marketing Systems, has developed a phenomenally successful multimedia marketing campaign used by thousands of restaurants, capturing and using the birthdays of every customer. This works because nobody celebrates a birthday alone, and the number one way birthdays are celebrated is going out to a restaurant. Each birthday brings two to eight people in the door. This is very reliable. Name the type of restaurant, and the owner can tell you what each birthday on file is worth in dollars, year after year. So let's say a birthday captured is worth $100.00 a year to restaurant owner, Bob. Now at the end of the night, Bob has a deposit for his Present Bank Account *and* another deposit for his Future Bank Account. For his Present Bank Account, the night's revenues of $20.00 times 200 diners, $4,000.00 less costs, equals $2,000.00. But his wait staff also collected names, e-mail addresses, addresses, and birthdays from 37 first-time customers. Bob deposits $3,700.00 in his Future Bank Account.

It is this operating principle that built up the wealth in my business over a 15-year period. For example, every time I got on an airplane and schlepped somewhere to speak, I made $10,000.00 or $20,000.00 or $30,000.00 from the fee, plus the books and courses sold, less my costs of goods, travel, overhead, to deposit in my Present Bank Account. But in my business, each newly acquired customer was known to be worth thousands of dollars in Future Bank value. So every day, my Future Bank deposit was much, much larger than my Present Bank deposit.

So it stacked up year after year. As it peaked, I was able to extract millions from my businesses and also sell my businesses.

To the degree that the Future Bank value of whatever you do today matches or exceeds the Present Bank value, you set in motion wealth *creation* forces that will soon deliver a massive harvest. Further, when you see your Future Bank balance building exponentially, your sense of being wealthy grows, and that sense or (mental) state of being wealthy *attracts* more wealth. A big, accurately, and legitimately calculated Future Bank balance has all the same positive effects as does or would an equally large Present Bank balance. You think differently, feel differently, speak differently, act differently, and are perceived more favorably by others when you are wealthy, secure, and independent than when you are not. Your Future Bank balance can give this to you faster.

Wealth Magnet 22
Marketing Prowess

Here is THE secret of secrets about the entrepreneurs who create and attract great wealth with relative ease, and are sought after by other wealthy entrepreneurs, executives, and investors who are eager to do business with them.

These superentrepreneurs may not be able to find their car keys, keep their offices free of overwhelming clutter, read balance sheets, or turn on computers. What they *don't* know would shock most people. Their personality flaws and personal dysfunctions could keep teams of psychotherapists gainfully employed. But one thing is true of virtually every single one of them: they are unabashed, unashamed, irrepressible promoters.

They are salespeople who know how to sell and do so day in and day out, and understand and usually keep their hands firmly on their firms' marketing. They are first and foremost marketers.

> Frankly, if you have emotional hang-ups about sales and marketing, don't "like" it, are convinced you aren't good at it, and refuse to hunker down and get good at it, I just don't have much hope for you when it comes to wealth attraction.

Some entrepreneurs good at other things try delegating all of the marketing. I've yet to see that go well. I see them delegate just about everything else with liveable results, but not the marketing.

I'll tell you an instructive story. For about a year, I had a very major corporation, owned by a big global conglomerate, as a client. You'd know the names. The CEO was a pleasant fellow good at holding meetings, counting the beans, and managing. But he was totally clueless about how to get customers. The company's several hundred franchisees wanted to lynch him. Its ad agency was scamming him. One day, he sat down with me in his office, door firmly closed, and told me he'd run some numbers and was distressed to discover that I was being paid a big multiple of what he was being paid, on an hourly basis—"and, after all," he said, "I am the CEO here."

I said, "That's okay. There's a very good reason why you're paying me so much more per hour than you can pay yourself. You know how to do everything here far better than I do, maybe better than anybody else, except for one little thing. I know how to get customers for you. You don't. Without what I know, everything you know is worthless. But, don't let this worry you. We'll keep this our little secret."

Here's the undeniable fact about my wealth: people have been attracted to me, line up and literally wait and beg and compete for my attention, and stay glued to me if they can for one reason and one reason only. It's not my warm 'n fuzzy personality. It's because I know how to get customers for them. I see opportunities in their businesses that they are blind to. So they tolerate my quirks and unusual demands and business practices. They pay very high fees and stay even when I raise fees with impunity. If you know marketing, you are in the ultimate power position.

Arnold Schwarzenegger got a part he wanted, over the strident objections of the director, because the studio heads knew no other star knew how to promote a movie like Arnold. They told the director if it's you or him who has to go, it will be you. That's how it works in the real world. The least dispensable person with the most power is the person who can bring in money. *The Apprentice* became an astounding TV success and, behind the scenes, an enormous financial success for NBC, Mark Burnett, and Trump not only because it was a great show (it was) but more because Donald Trump is an incredible, relentless promoter. I recently had a client, who must remain nameless, sell his company for an outrageous 15-times multiple of earnings because the bigger competitor was simply worn out and frustrated with competing with his superior marketing. They paid just to make him stop.

Every entrepreneur I know who has "money magnetism" also has exceptional marketing prowess.

*O*ther books in the No B.S. series are *No B.S. Direct Marketing for NON-Direct Marketing Businesses* and *No B.S. Sales Success*, from bookstores or online booksellers. Additional information at www.nobs books.com. Also, enter the National Sales Letter/ Marketing Plan Contest, compete for a new Ford Mustang and other awards, and enroll in free marketing e-courses at www.NationalSalesLetterContest.com. Read *The Ultimate Marketing Plan* and *The Ultimate Sales Letter* also by this author.

Wealth Magnet 23
Behavioral Congruency

Behavioral Congruency is the core idea behind my entire "Renegade Millionaire System."

It is a deceptively simple idea, contrary to the overwhelming majority of self-improvement and success literature. It doesn't negate anything in any of the thousands of other how-to-succeed or how-to-get-rich books, courses, or seminars, but I do say it is more important than anything in those books.

Most approaches to becoming more successful or prosperous focus on attitudes and thoughts. But, as a result of 30 years' work with well over 100 first-generation, from-scratch millionaire and multimillionaire entrepreneurs and my current work with so many million-dollar-a-year earners and wealthy entrepreneurs, I came to one major conclusion:

It's less about how they *think* than about what they *do.*

Just for example, I worked 12 hours today, on a Sunday, on this book. I didn't wake up highly motivated to do that. I wasn't inspired by a muse. Nor did I try to get inspired or motivated or find somebody to motivate me. I didn't need a motivational tape. I didn't waste even a minute trying to modify my attitude. *I just went to work* and wrote because I had an imminent deadline and I prize keeping my commitments above just about everything else. That's what I do. I work to meet deadlines. This is all about behavior, not positive thinking.

Sure, that's little more than self-imposed, situation-imposed discipline. But there's another layer that goes on top of this that's even more important. Step 1 is Behavior, but advanced wealth attraction Step 2 is Congruent Behavior.

Step 1: Behavior
Step 2: Congruent Behavior

Congruent with *what*?

First—and this is key—*congruent with the behavior of people already achieving the goals you want to achieve,* already living the kind of life you want to live. This is called "modeling." Find them, study them, model them. And model their behavior. Don't worry too much about their thinking or attitudes. It's what they do and how they do it that matters most.

If your behavior is incongruent with the behavior of the people who enjoy the kinds of successes you aspire to, you can't get those kinds of successes. A simple example: top golfers use great coaches and practice regularly and frequently. If you are too cheap to get a great coach or too lazy or busy to practice, you can forget about being a top golfer. And you can "be motivated" and "think positive" and "visualize" all you want, bubba, but you still ain't going to be a top golfer!

On the other hand, the quicker you align your present behavior with the behavior of people who already have, are achieving, and are experiencing the results you aspire to, the faster you get those results. In fact, the result will so closely follow the behavior alignment that it will seem instant.

Second, *be congruent with the goals themselves.* Consider a goal to lose 40 pounds. Dropping by the doughnut shop every morning is incongruent behavior. Stocking your pantry with cookies, incongruent. Going out with friends to a place that only serves pizza, incongruent. Taking the elevator up to the second floor instead of walking up the stairs, incongruent. The quicker you rearrange your behaviors to be congruent with the goal, the quicker you get the goal.

Most people are, bluntly, bullshitters—b.s.ing themselves! What could be worse than lying to yourself? But if you claim a goal but behave in ways incongruent with the goal, you're a b.s.er.

With regard to wealth, if you get your behavior congruent with whatever your wealth goals are and congruent with the behavior of others who've achieved your wealth goals, it is an absolute certainty your wealth will come flowing in—probably faster than you would have imagined. In fact, there is a thing I

> "*B*y following your behavioral goals, you get to your objectives.
>
> "Instead of trying to break par, a result we cannot control, we concentrate on putting a good swing on the ball, an action we can control. The distinction is crystal clear, surely, but it never ceases to amaze me that the same folks in my workshops who nod their heads in agreement with the golf analogy turn right around and announce that their goal in this negotiation is to sign the deal and collect the money. So I ask you again, is this signing and collecting something you can actually control?. . . what you can control is behavior and activity, what you cannot control is the result of this behavior and activity.
>
> "Think behavior, forget result."
>
> —JIM CAMP, AMERICA'S #1 NEGOTIATING COACH AND AUTHOR OF *START WITH NO*, WWW.CAMPMETHOD.COM

call "The Phenomenon." Every wealthy entrepreneur I work with has experienced it at least once, most several times in their lives. Personally, it's been three times for me, including right now. The Phenomenon is when you accomplish more or attract more wealth in 12 months than in the previous 6 years, or some similar amazing ratio. For most, The Phenomenon seems to just happen.

Most think, "finally!" But The Phenomenon can actually be made to happen, can be helped along and accelerated, because it is little more than a reflection of both kinds of Behavioral Congruency converging. You can't directly make The Phenomenon happen, but you can make Behavioral Congruency happen.

The more aligned you are with the things you want,
the more powerfully you attract them.

The things you *congruently* want have no choice
but to be attracted to you.

People who are *congruent* are attractive,
magnetic—even charismatic.

When you are *fully* congruent,
you are irresistible.

—Mark Victor Hansen,
co-author of *Chicken Soup for the Soul* and
Robert Allen, author of *Nothing Down* and *Creating Wealth*
from their book, *The One-Minute Millionaire*
www.oneminutemillionaire.com
www.markvictorhansen.com

Wealth Magnet 24
Act Wealthy to Attract Wealth

There are actually *two* Wealth Magnets here, and one will seem obvious and logical, but the other will seem completely illogical and be very difficult to accept. It usually takes hours to present properly, and the equal of that in pages just isn't available here. So I can only caution you against using one Magnet without the other and encourage you to try *The 90-Day Experiment* that I suggest here. You need not have any confidence in its working for it to work. You only need to do it for 90 days. You'll see results. You'll be amazed. Then you'll stick with it even though you may never be able to logically explain it to anyone else, just as I can't logically explain it to you.

First, let's talk about what I'm NOT talking about here: "act as if." In a lot of "wealth seminars," the speakers encourage you to buy new clothes, new cars, a mansion, start living the lifestyle of the rich and famous, and essentially pretend to be rich, somehow fooling yourself and others. Their idea is "pretend and money will follow." Actually, most people experience "pretend and bankruptcy will follow." However, they are onto something when it comes to fooling your subconscious. If you act in the same ways that the wealthy act, you set in motion a big collection of internal changes and external effects that do attract wealth. It so happens I know hundreds of very wealthy people intimately, almost all first-generation rich, entrepreneurs who've made it from scratch. A few are "new money flashy"—private jets, big mansions, bling bling. Most are not. Most behave more like the millionaires described in detail by Thomas Stanley in *The Millionaire Next Door* and his other research. But there are two things all really wealthy people do that you can mimic and that will have surprisingly dramatic, positive, wealth attracting effects.

The logical one is saving. Systematic, disciplined saving. This is important because wealth is not about income. Most people focus only on increasing income. But the wealthy are just as concerned or more concerned with increasing equity. So, here's The 90-Day Experiment. Immediately establish a new bank account, and call it your Wealth Account. It can be checking, interest bearing checking, or money market. At first, it doesn't matter. Next, determine a fixed percentage of every dollar that comes your way that will be diverted into that Wealth Account. Something between 1% and 10%. You may think you can't do this—hey, I can't pay my bills now with 100% of every buck; how will I pay them with 90%? Well, maybe you won't. But you aren't now either! So just do it. Pick a percentage, deposit the money, and then do NOT touch it, no matter what. And make these deposits every time a dollar arrives. Daily if need be. The more often the better. The act of putting money into your Wealth Account does things to and through your subconscious mind that cannot be fully explained. The amount matters a lot less than the act. You could be poor, getting paid $10.00 a day, decide on 1%, and be putting only 10 cents a day into a piggy bank. Even though you would directly accumulate little in 90 days, so many other things would change in your life, you'd still be amazed.

If you feel like reading about the core practicality of this, try the classic book *Richest Man in Babylon* by George Clason.

Anyway, make a deposit to your Wealth Account of a predetermined percentage of EVERY dollar you receive.

If you do take money out during The 90-Day Experiment, you MUST limit it to true investment. If, for example, you are paying a home mortgage or auto loan and have enough in the Wealth Account to pay an extra monthly principal payment, that's acceptable. But it's NOT to pay your regular monthly payment. That's not kosher.

Now here comes the completely illogical one: giving. This is important because all wealthy people give. Giving has an incredible effect on your psyche. So, immediately open another separate bank account and call it your "Giving Account." Again, predetermine a fixed percentage of every dollar that you receive to divert to your Giving Account. There, you will build up amounts to give to your charities, churches, people in need, even over-tip hard working people. If you take money out during The 90-Day Experiment, which I encourage, it must be to give away with no direct quid pro quo or expectation of return

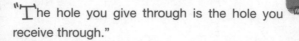

"The hole you give through is the hole you receive through."

—DR. EDWARD KRAMER, AUTHOR AND CREATOR OF
"SYNCHROMATICS" AND INVENTOR OF THE "THANK-U-GRAM"

or gain, and it should not replace giving you already do, such as whatever you now drop into the church collection plate every Sunday.

Obviously, it's hard to imagine how SUBTRACTING 10% from your income and giving it away can increase your income or wealth: 100% minus 10% = 90% and $10,000.00 minus $1,000.00 = $9,000.00. But, somehow, this math works more like this: 100% − 10% = 100% x 4 = 400%.

The first time I heard this from Foster Hibbard, I thought he was nutty as my grandmother's fruitcake. I don't blame you for thinking I'm smoking crack. But I assure you, try it for 90 days, and you'll be a convert.

Later, by the way, you can get more sophisticated. Your Wealth Account money can move through the account into various investments. Personally, for my Giving Account, I use a charitable trust account with Fidelity Investments that puts the money in my choice of Fidelity funds, dispenses donations as I direct, and provides the charitable tax deduction the year I deposit the funds whether they are dispensed that same year or not. Others create their own foundations. There are also complex issues, like donation of appreciated assets free of capital gains taxes. But all that can wait. First, run The 90-Day Experiment.

The Power of Habitforce

We *are* creatures of habit.

You probably do your morning regimen the same way every morning by habit. Drive to certain destinations the same way every time by habit. Maybe have exactly the same argument with spouse or friend again and again by habit. You either leave the toothpaste tube cap off or put it on by habit.

By adopting, installing, and controlling certain "habits of wealthy entrepreneurs," you put habitforce on your side, as a means of naturally attracting wealth. Napoleon Hill discovered such habits in common in the hundreds of exceptional entrepreneurs and achievers he researched and interviewed from 1917 to 1935, in preparation for the publication of his works, *Laws of Success* and *Think and Grow Rich*. In my more up-close, personal, intense, and involved work with over 100 from-scratch millionaire and multimillionaire entrepreneurs, I have also observed certain habits in common. Hundreds of differences but a few habits held in common.

Two habits are almost universal in these wealthy entrepreneurs. No, most do not do them as mechanically and rigidly as I have described here, although quite a few did when they adopted the habits at my suggestion. I am more flexible with myself now and tend to make Wealth deposits only a few times a month and Giving deposits the same. And I actually no longer have a single Wealth Account and, instead, track it all on paper in a mythical account summarizing all my investments. But in the beginning, I made my deposits religiously, frequently, every time money arrived, exactly as Foster described to me.

Wealth Magnet 25
Energy from People

There are very practical obstacles to wealth attraction that short-circuit your wealth attraction.

The first big obstacle is incompetent people. Sometimes, these are people incapable of handling the responsibilities or doing the jobs entrusted to them. More frequently, these are people able but unwilling to do the jobs. They are lazy and uncreative. They are absent a sense of urgency or initiative, so they will do only the minimum, they will not figure out solutions, and they will let their progress be stalled by the slightest challenge and return everything to your lap. Dealing with such people is simply a miserable, sadly common experience. Every entrepreneur wrestles with these people. They may be employees, vendors, advisors, or others.

Another related obstacle is people who waste or abuse your time, what I call "time vampires." This bunch can just as easily include certain clients or customers as employees and vendors.

Another, related obstacle is people who drain or divert your mental energy, who disrupt the flow of your wealth attraction. Negative people, gloom 'n doom people, whiners, and complainers. Mike Vance, former Dean of Disney University, calls them pissers and moaners. This bunch can just as easily include friends and relatives as well as employees, vendors, customers, or clients.

They must all go. The minute you detect their toxic odor, take action to get them out of your business, out of your life, and to distance yourself from them. You need to develop a Zero Tolerance Policy about all these people and be decisive, even ruthless, in enforcing it. Hesitancy and timidity in doing so will always cost you more than whatever temporary trauma and disruption results from making changes in your staff, vendors, or others around you. Always.

I'll give you a very common example. A client with five staff members in his office brought me in to observe, interview, analyze, and look at his business from top to bottom with my "fresh eyes." I told him that his majorette domo, his key office manager, and the employee with him the longest, had to go. I told him she was sabotaging his new initiatives behind his back, ignoring procedures he wanted followed, damaging morale, and driving away good clients. I told him she was the equal of an open vat of toxic chemicals. He insisted he needed her, relied on her, and couldn't function without her; at bare minimum, the disruption caused by firing her would be disastrous. It took me over a year to convince him to give the old battleax the ax. Immediately after doing so, sales increased. No other changes. No increased advertising. Her exit, enter more income. Within the year, the business was 30% more profitable, the remaining employees measurably more productive, and my client happier, more relaxed, and more productive. By the following year, his net worth had increased by nearly $500,000.00, and he had enough liberated time to finally launch a second business he'd been back-burnering for years. A "wealth block" had been surgically removed and vibrant health created by its removal.

Think of your wealth attraction power as electric current. Years ago, strings of Christmas lights could be short-circuited by any loose bulb, any burnt out bulb, or any bad fuse. If there was one of these anywhere in the entire string of lights, it disrupted the flow of power, and the entire string shut off. I remember helping my father unscrew and test bulb after bulb, fuse after fuse, to find the one bad one. The power cord that runs between you and the world supply of wealth and the world supply of wealth and you has a very similar flaw. One disruptive person laying a finger on it anywhere along the line shuts down the entire flow of power.

I try my level best to operate a Zero Tolerance Policy toward people who disrupt the flow of my wealth attraction power. Be they employee, vendor, associate, or client, I will not tolerate interference with the flow of wealth to me. I rid myself of them, even if at considerable, temporary cost. I have, on several occasions, stopped projects for clients after I'd done a lot of work on them, refunded as much as $70,000.00, just to get rid of the client who was a "problem child," seriously interfering with my flow of power.

One of my rules:

> If I wake up *three* morn-ings *thinking about you* and I'm *not having sex with you,* you've got to go.

Most people tolerate others causing them undue stress and aggravation, without realizing how costly such tolerance is. I want you to understand: it is very, very costly.

The opposite of all this is the assembly and organization of your own small cadre of exceptionally competent, highly creative, extraordinarily reliable, and trustworthy individuals who are in sync and harmony with you and your objectives, who facilitate and even multiply your wealth attraction power. If you read Lee Iacocca's autobiography, you saw his description of this as his "horses," the few key people he relied on. If you carefully observed Donald Trump during his *Apprentice* television programs, read his books, and read the biography about him, you realized that George and Carolyn and several other key people make Trump possible. Without them, Trump wouldn't be and couldn't be Trump. You will find this theme true of all incredibly accomplished, successful, and wealthy entrepreneurs.

In short, the people around you, the people who populate your world, the people you rely on either enhance or sap your wealth attraction power. No person with whom you interact is a neutral factor. Each and every person either drains power from you or contributes power to you. One or the other. Power source or power drain. Ally or enemy. Black or white.

Refusing to face the black and white nature of this with clarity and accuracy and honesty is a major obstacle to wealth attraction. Refusing to act appropriately and decisively about what you deduce about a person, about a power drainer, is a major obstacle to wealth attraction.

How to Build a "Power Team" Around You

I have been very, very fortunate in my life to have had a number of people around me who have added to my power. They have changed over time; some left, some come. Change is inevitable. But I have certainly had an enormous amount of support.

Mine is in tiers.

In the first tier have been spouses, close associates, close friends, people I've relied on heavily, at different times, in different ways. My second wife, Carla, for example, was an important, chief source of support and power for many of the 22 years of our marriage. At present, Bill Glazer, who publishes my *No B.S. Marketing Letter* and operates Glazer-Kennedy Inner Circle, and his crackerjack staff, and Pete Lillo, who publishes two of my other newsletters, are enormously valuable business associates I can rely on without equivocation. Vicky Tolleson, my lone employee, office manager, personal assistant, time and access sentry, problem solver, and client services director, is valuable beyond description. These people and a very short list of others, past or present, work with me pretty much on my terms, with the prime purpose of supporting and facilitating my productivity.

They view their responsibility and best interests as making it possible for me to function at peak performance. I also have a very short list of people I can rely on for advice, counsel, and information. It features Lee Milteer, a close friend and associate, who is a reliable sounding board, encourager, but also questioner. The total number of people in this tier at any given time is less than a dozen.

In the second tier are both suppliers and clients. For example, for nine years, I've run a formal "mastermind group" exclusively for information marketers in businesses akin to my own, all highly successful and innovative, all wealthy. While they pay me well to organize, host, facilitate, and direct the group and its meetings, I also participate as a member and benefit from the exchange of ideas and information. This tier also includes my CPA firm, the person I am most involved with in real estate investments, Darin Garman, and other paid advisors.

In the third tier are all the other clients I work with, the other vendors I rely on, the other sources of information I access, and trade associations I belong to. Included here, for example, is the publisher of this book, its editor, its marketing people, my other publishers, my literary agents, and my publicist. Also included are the consulting and copywriting clients I work for and who support me, but who I must still act discriminately toward. Also included are the editors, graphic artists, web masters, and other professionals and vendors I use intermittently, project by project.

This is "Planet Dan," a world I create and own and control, populated only by people I permit to be there, governed by laws I legislate and enforce. It's a small planet, so I have some level of personal relationship with every inhabitant of the planet. Every one of these relationships is a two-way street. They all influence me as I influence them. That's unavoidable. They all either enhance or drain my energy. They all either support and facilitate or interfere with my productivity. They all either enhance or disrupt my wealth attraction.

This is true of every single person you permit existence in your world, too. Rule *your* world accordingly.

Another book in the No B.S. Series is *No B.S. Time Management for Entrepreneurs*, essential reading on the subject of governing your world! Available in bookstores or from online booksellers. Additional information at www.nobsbooks.com.

Wealth Magnet 26
Courage

I have an unpublished book I've been working on, off, and on for years with the words "brass balls" in its title. The publishers I've approached lack the brass balls to publish it! You can, however, get the gist of its 300-page message just from those two words. The meek may inherit the earth, but not anytime soon. *Fortune favors the bold. Courage attracts wealth.*

You have to put yourself out there.

I'm not talking about taking unbridled financial risk, although from time to time, you do have to put some chips on the table. This is about your ego, self-esteem, reputation, relationships, dealing with the ever-present *what will he/she/they think of me?*

"You don't need experience to do many things. You can learn as you go along."

—GENE SIMMONS, MEMBER OF THE BAND KISS
AND AUTHOR OF *SEX, MONEY, KISS*

You need courage to act on your ideas. Courage to defy conventional wisdom or even the expert advice you solicit when you believe your ideas are best. Courage to start before you are ready, to fumble around in the dark, to screw up. Courage to face embarrassment, humiliation, rejection. Courage to stand by your convictions. Courage to make demands, to set rules and boundaries, to define the way you will do business, and to impose your will on the world around you. Courage to end unproductive relationships and fire uncooperative employees or clients. Courage to wrest control of your time from everyone around you. Courage to define and pursue goals. Courage to ask, to promote, to sell aggressively, forcefully, noisily, visibly. Courage to ignore criticism, to focus on results.

Wealth rarely rewards wimps.

In an ethereal sense, I think wealth is waiting, watching the entrepreneur, holding back a while, just to see how big his brass balls are (or how small). At some point, wealth's admiration, even lust for the incredibly strong, certain, unwavering, resilient entrepreneur, boils over and wealth comes flowing toward the entrepreneur, wealth gives herself up totally and completely. (Need a cold shower?)

There are very real forces that govern the movement of money. Money doesn't move around from one person to another by fate, accident, luck. It moves for reasons, in response to magnetic forces. Money moves because of Authority—that's why experts get rich, why the top cardiac surgeon at Cleveland Clinic is so much wealthier than the generalist M.D. just down the street. Money moves with Transfer of Responsibility—that's how financial planners and advisors, brokers and money managers get rich. Money moves on a base level because of Value Exchange. But most of all, it is my understanding that money moves because of Courage.

"I can zero in on a vision of where I want to be in the future. I can see it so clearly in front of me, when I daydream, it's almost a reality. Then I get this easy feeling, and I don't have to be uptight to get there because I already feel like I'm there, that it's just a matter of time."

"I set a goal, visualized it very clearly, then created the drive, the hunger for turning it into a reality. There's a kind of joy in that kind of ambition, in having a vision in front of you. With that kind of joy, discipline isn't difficult or negative or grim. You love doing what you have to do—going to the gym, working hard on the set. Even when pain is part of reaching your goal, and it usually is, you can accept that too."

—Arnold Schwarzenegger

BONUS CHAPTERS
FROM GUEST EXPERTS

Introduction from
Dan Kennedy

I have never claimed to be an investment, finance, or wealth management expert. In fact, for too many years of my life I was as guilty as most entrepreneurs of over-emphasizing the making of money and paying too little attention to investing, preserving, and multiplying money. My own personal shift from merely being a high-income entrepreneur to a high-income and wealthy entrepreneur has only occurred in the last ten years or so, thanks in part to the influence and assistance of "specialists" in different aspects of investment and finance. I have some relationship with the experts presented here. They are clients of mine: Some are in my mastermind groups where I benefit from their ideas and information as they do from mine. Some provide advice or services to me or my other clients. They were each hand-picked by me because they bring a different viewpoint and a different opportunity, as well as authority, expertise, and experience to the total discussion of wealth.

Including them here does not transfer any liability or responsibility to me or this book's publisher for any decisions you make, actions you take, or relationships you enter into because each individual's circumstances are different. You are 100% responsible for your own financial and business decisions. If unwilling to accept such responsibility, you should read no further. And, should you be in doubt about any investment-related decision or similar matter, the counsel and services of appropriate professionals, such as your own CPA or attorney, should be sought.

My long-time friend Dr. Herb True, for many years a business professor at Notre Dame, once told me that many students were confused when he assigned multiple books with contradictory or varied viewpoints on the same subject. They wanted him to tell him which one was *the* right book. Regrettably, the subject of money is not so simple. Each person is at a different place in age, experience, income, wealth, available time, risk tolerance, initiative, interest in active or passive investments, etc., and each individual must think independently and arrive at his own way, the way right for him.

Not long ago, I had a one-day consultation with Somers White, someone I occasionally look to for advice on business and financial matters. Somers and I have known each other for many years. He lives in Phoenix, where I lived for about 20 years, and he and I are both speakers and members of the National Speakers

Association. His rich business background includes a stint as a bank president, and he is extremely astute on financial issues affecting entrepreneurs and family businesses. For about half of this day, we reviewed my complete, current business and personal financial position, objectives, and plan for my remaining few years of active work before my early retirement. I pointed out that most financial professionals and advisors would argue with my chosen strategies. I was really looking for a sanity check-up. A session like this is the financial equivalent of stripping naked for a physical, one that includes an invasive procedure or two. Afterwards, you feel like you should cough. Anyway, his conclusion was, "While it might not be correct or best for others, your strategy and plan is perfect for you."

In this section, you will discover experts, opportunities, and opinions—including a few opinions not in perfect harmony with everything I've said in the first section. All of it is for the purpose of stimulating you to think—not to tell you what to think!

When I first started in public speaking, I was advised not to talk about sex, politics, or religion, never to follow an animal act, and never to actually ask an audience to think. I have violated every one of those suggestions. As I do here.

Who Else Wants to Be a *Real* Real Estate Millionaire?

Thad Winston

E ven if you do not own any real estate other than your own home, you undoubtedly have a relative, friend, or neighbor who is an investor. More than one third of all homes bought and sold in America in 2004/2005 were sold or bought by investors. There's a good reason you see so much advertising and hype about this subject. Done right, it works! Real estate can be the most controllable, predictable, safe, and secure way to invest your money, leverage your money, and multiply wealth. It is part of just about every wealthy individual's or family's investment portfolio. It can also be a great entrepreneurial opportunity.

But you may be thinking, "Yeah, but it takes a lot of money . . . . too much time . . . risk . . . you need great credit . . . . there are all of the hassles of dealing with tenants . . . . it's a lot harder than it looks."

My own experience says you're wrong. I am a successful insurance agent with a name-brand company. I do well financially in my business. But I actually make a lot more money on the side, from my real estate investments. And although I am busy with my insurance business full-time, I find it easy to more than triple my income in my spare time through real estate. Oh, and I started when I did not have good credit—in fact, I'd been through bankruptcy!

Of course, it's possible to make costly mistakes, to wind up buried in landlord headaches, or to wind up with negative cash flow. I'd be a liar if I tried to paint a picture of roses with no thorns, a paved highway straight to millions with no bumps or potholes. That's why it's so important to find an experienced mentor and coach and to determine which of the many different ways to passively invest or to be actively involved as an entrepreneur in real estate, as I am.

Who Should Be Doing Real Estate Deals?

In my opinion, just about everybody! Maybe you. Lots of people with very, very successful businesses make the time to learn real estate and to do deals because it is so lucrative. There is some opportunity right for everybody. If you're just looking for stable, predictable monthly income to offset ups and downs in your business, real estate investing can provide the answer. If you're looking for a way to make a lot of money in a hurry, to supplement your income, or to create money outside your regular business to pour 100% into wealth accumulation, then doing the kinds of real estate deals I do may be your answer.

In this brief chapter, I thought I'd show you two of my favorite "Shortcuts to Real Estate Profits" that I use and teach to the students I mentor.

Shortcut Strategy 1: Get a Deed for Free!

Getting a deed "subject to mortgage" is so easy my 13-year-old daughter could do it, if it were legal for her to sign contracts. Here's all there is to it.

"Subject to mortgage" means you get the deed to the house and the seller keeps the mortgage in his name. Ultimately, you can extract profits without ever making an out-of-pocket investment. Here's an actual example from Bill Skerbetz, a coaching client of mine in Pennsylvania.

A homeowner responded to one of the ads I gave Bill to run. Dean, the homeowner, had just gone through a nasty, lengthy divorce, and he was newly engaged to another woman. Dean's new fiancée hated the old house and insisted they move immediately, so Dean was paying rent where they lived and making the mortgage payments on the vacant house.

Bill explained how he could solve Dean's problem quickly. Dean deeded the house to Bill and paid Bill $1,800.00 to cover the next three month's mortgage payments. Bill agreed to find a tenant-buyer to rent-to-own the house, relieving Dean of the mortgage liability. The house also needed some minor repairs, and real estate agents had told Dean he needed to make them all before listing the house. Then who could guess how long it would take to get it sold? Dean's fiancée wanted no part of putting more money into the old house, and Dean was strapped for cash anyway. He owed $62,700.00 on the house.

In less than 45 days, Bill sold the house for $109,900.00. He got a check for $26,223.00 plus the $1,800.00 he got from Dean. Bill was able to convert the person who responded to his rent-to-own advertising into a buyer immediately, using strategies I teach. Bill helped the buyer qualify for a loan for 90% of the purchase price, and he carried a small second mortgage, which pays him a monthly income.

Because Bill had almost no money out of his pocket in this deal, his return on investment is, well, infinite! Dean and his fiancée were thrilled to get out from under the mortgage and the uncertainty and hassle of trying to sell the home, the new buyers were happy to own a home (when they thought they couldn't), and Bill was happy with profits of more than $20,000.00, with less than ten hours' time and almost no money invested.

Laws about "subject to mortgage" and rent-to-own or lease option arrangements may vary state to state, and there is a little bit you need to learn about doing this. But you can see from this example it is basically simple. What may surprise you is just how many Dean's there are out there who are willing, eager, and happy to walk away from whatever equity might be in their home in exchange for a fast, simple, easy exit from a mortgage they can't handle.

Shortcut Strategy 2: Finder's Fees

Have you ever introduced a person you know to a different person? Played matchmaker? That's how simple it is to pocket finder's fees in my world.

You find "ugly ducklings." These are houses that need a lot of repairs and can be bought at a good price. These kinds of properties are ideal for investors who like doing rehab work—and there are a lot of them. Often, the type of person who enjoys rehabbing houses does not enjoy going out, finding, and negotiating deals. If you will find properties, you'll never need to get your hands dirty or pick up a hammer to make a lot of money.

Rehab investors can make a lot of money on a property. In my experience, they'll usually make $20,000.00 to $30,000.00 in profit on each house, so they don't mind paying you a small finder's fee.

How do you find rehab investors? Here's one of my best tricks. Step 1 is simply to run a small ad like this under "Houses for Sale": Handyman Special, Cheap for Cash Buyer. Run it with your phone number. When you get calls, keep the names and phone numbers of the people you identify as investors able to pay cash, who want fixer-uppers, and tell them you'll call them as soon as your next property is available. Step 2 is to find the vacant or run-down house, negotiate with the owner, and get the house under contract at a good price. Step 3 is to call your ugly duckling investors, send them to look at the house, and invite bids, starting at $5,000.00 more than the price you negotiated. Step 4 is to take the highest bidder. Do what's called a "simultaneous closing," with the homeowner in one room, the investor in the other. Step 5 is to take your profit of $5,000.00 or more.

There are lots of people who get started in real estate entrepreneuring this way. And I know people, including people I coach and mentor, making $100,000.00 to $250,000.00 a year just doing this—part-time!

Incidentally, in case you didn't know it, you can use your own IRA or Roth-IRA to do these kinds of real estate deals, with all the profits going into your IRA tax-free until you later withdraw them. This is a great way to grow your retirement savings, or to open a Roth-IRA for your son or daughter, and help them become wealthy, too.

Doing real estate deals like this is fun and profitable!

Thad Winston is a real estate investor, coach, and mentor to other investors and entrepreneurs, including beginners. For information about Thad's services, visit www.thadwinston.com.

Income for Life Buying and Holding Residential Real Estate
Rob Minton

I'm excited to show you a proven real estate investment method that consistently creates massive wealth and cash flow with minimal investment of time and money. I will outline the Income For Life System and show you how starting with one beautiful single-family home could potentially compound into 24 homes in less than seven short years without having to invest any additional money out of your pocket. And if that doesn't sound great enough, the best news is you'll only need a minimal amount of money to begin—as little as $5,000.00 (or less) is common! The Income For Life System has not only worked well for me personally, but it has also helped hundreds of my clients create wealth as well. This investing approach has lead many of us to achieve financial freedom in a very short time. Furthermore, many more beginners are well on their way to the same results.

First off, I have personally invested in commercial properties, multifamily properties, mobile homes, and single-family homes. I also am a real estate broker and specialize in helping investors acquire wealth. Over the years, I perfected a simple system for profiting from nice single-family homes. In fact, my clients who follow my simple Income For Life System lock in average profits of $28,071.00 on each single-family home they acquire.

The secret to creating real wealth, income, and cash flow in real estate is to learn how to increase the demand for a property. In all of the other investments that I have made personally, such as commercial properties or multifamily properties, I haven't been able to increase the demand as well as I have for single-family homes. As you already know, the more demand there is for something, the more people will pay for it. Just think of Donald Trump. He creates massive demand for his properties. He is a billionaire. Notice the correlation? Massive demand for your single-family homes can make you very wealthy in a short period of time.

Investing Approaches

There are basically two approaches to real estate investing—the "buy-and-hold strategy" and the "rehab-and-flip strategy." The buy-and-hold investor typically buys a property and holds it forever. He profits mainly from the appreciation of the property over time and the tax benefits of ownership. The main drawback to this approach is the limited cash flow. Home prices have increased and the monthly rents received barely cover the monthly mortgage, taxes, and insurance costs under the buy-and-hold strategy. The rehab-and-flip strategy, if successful, provides large pay days without any continuous monthly cash flow. I have figured out a way to maximize the benefits of both approaches while eliminating all of the ugly drawbacks of each. This blended approach creates both short-term and long-term returns by using "Rent To Own" programs.

Creating Demand

Here is an outline of how I use Rent To Own programs to create more demand, increase cash flow, and get large paydays. I buy a nice single-family home in a nice area, and I offer this home on a Rent To Own program. The nice home in the nice area is a very important concept, which I can't explain in this brief chapter. However, you definitely want to look for homes that a renter would really want to own, not just rent. This may require that you pay more for your investment properties. See Figure 1.

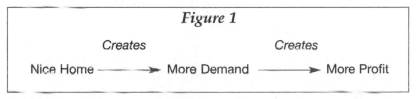

Figure 1

Creates   Creates

Nice Home ———▶ More Demand ———▶ More Profit

The main reason that I like to offer my single family homes on Rent To Own programs is to increase demand for my homes dramatically. The National Association of Realtors compiled a survey in 2003 that noted that 82% of all buyers purchased their homes simply because "they wanted to own their own homes." Americans have a dream of home ownership. When you combine this dream of home ownership with lenders telling renters that they do not qualify to buy a home, magic happens. You as an investor can put yourself in a position of selling food to a starving crowd. Many renters have issues in their credit scores that prevent them from qualifying to buy their own homes. If they do qualify, the lenders require 20% or 30% down. The majority of renters cannot afford a 20% down payment on a home. However, they can afford to pay $5,000.00 to $10,000.00 upfront for a home with a Rent To Own program. Figure 2 shows where the real demand kicks in:

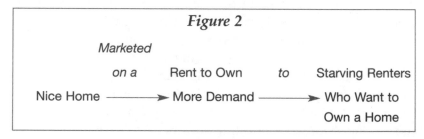

Figure 2

Marketed

on a   Rent to Own   to   Starving Renters

Nice Home ———▶ More Demand ———▶ Who Want to

Own a Home

When you offer a home that a tenant really would love to own on a Rent To Own program, demand skyrockets. In some situations, renters will literally fight over a nice Rent To Own home. High demand puts me in a position to collect large nonrefundable upfront payments from my new tenants who I refer to as Rent To Own buyers. A few weeks ago, we were offering a client's investment property on a Rent To Own program and received $9,000.00 upfront. My client received a check for $9,000.00 before the tenant even moved into his property. Large nonrefundable upfront payments are pure cash flow.

Psychology

Another key point for you to understand is the psychology of this program. If you are just renting your properties out to tenants, you are positioned as the landlord. However, when you sell your home to your Rent To Own buyer, you are positioned as a seller. When a tenant has a problem, whom do they give their problems to? The landlord. When a buyer has a problem, whom do they give their problems to? Themselves. This simple shift has tremendous benefits to you as the investor. See Figure 3.

Figure 3

Landlord/Tenant	Rent to Own Seller/Buyer
1. Landlord has MORE risk because he is only receiving a small security deposit.	1. Seller has LESS risk because he is receiving large upfront payments.
2. Landlord is responsible for majority of repairs and maintenance.	2. Seller is only responsible for certain repairs and maintenance.
3. Tenant doesn't care about the property; his mindset Is, "It's just a rental."	3. Buyer cares a great deal about the home; his mindset is, "This is my home!"
4. Tenant pays lower rent and moves more frequently. (Short-term leases)	4. Buyer pays a higher monthly rent and signs a longer-term lease with money to lose.

Hassle-Free Ownership

In fact, I strive to have my tenants manage the properties them-selves. I don't want to manage my properties; it isn't a good use of time. The agreements we sign with our Rent To Own buyers lay this out in detail by specifying that the buyer is responsible for making routine repairs to the property. Because we are invest-ing in nice homes, we rarely have large repairs eating up our cash flow. (Some examples of the contracts, forms, and agreements we use are included in my Income For Life System, which can be found at www.QuitWorkSomeDay.com/wealth.)

Higher Cash Flow

With our Rent To Own programs, we are able to charge higher monthly rents for our properties. Over the years, we have devel-oped what I refer to as an "Upsell Strategy." Using this strategy, you can charge an extra $150.00 to $250.00 a month in rent. Right when the prospective tenant falls in love with the home, you ask them to pay a higher monthly rent. Every penny of this higher monthly rent is free cash flow to you because it is above and beyond the normal market value rent you would have received.

Real Life Example

Here's an example of a home my Income For Life Member of the Year, Joe Mercadente, purchased.

University Heights, Ohio	
For the property, Joe paid:	$164,000.00
Upfront payment from tenant:	$9,000.00
Positive monthly cash flow:	$300.00 per month
Contract sale price to tenant:	$194,900.00
Total locked in profit on investment:	$38,100.00

My Income For Life System members also have special access to a 5% down investment loan program. If you were to use this loan program to purchase this home, your down payment would be approximately $8,2000.00. When comparing the upfront payment received from the Rent to Own buyer of $9,000.00 to the down payment of $8,200.00, you will notice that you would have actually been paid $800.00 to buy this home. In addition, you would receive a monthly positive cash flow of $300.00 for two years putting a total of $7,200.00 in your pocket. If your Rent To Own buyer bought out the home at the end of the Rent To Own program, you would put an additional $21,900.00 in your pocket ($194,900.00 minus $164,000.00 minus $9,000.00 upfront payments).

Now here is where the real wealth is created. Most investors would take the $21,900.00 profit when the property sells to their Rent To Own buyer and live off of it. They would either buy an expensive toy (new car, boat, motorcycle), or they would use it for their day-to-day living expenses. However, in my opinion, you should never take your money out of play. Once you have money invested in income producing assets, always keep that money invested in income producing assets. Live off of the cash flow from the properties, not the sales proceeds. I teach my Income For Life System members to use the sales proceeds for down payments on multiple properties. In the above property, Joe could take his proceeds and use them as a down payment on two more properties. Figure 5 shows what this would look like.

Offer these two new properties on Rent To Own programs, and collect two more upfront payments. Let's say that you were to receive $5,000.00 upfront from both of the new investments; this would put an additional $10,000.00 into your pocket. The cash flow from the first home was $800.00 plus the $7,200.00 for

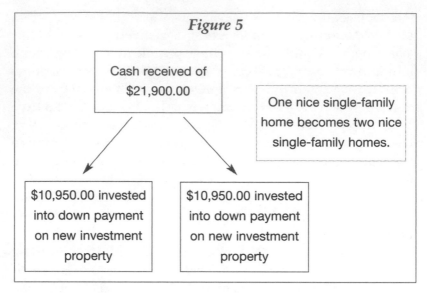

Figure 5

Cash received of $21,900.00

One nice single-family home becomes two nice single-family homes.

$10,950.00 invested into down payment on new investment property

$10,950.00 invested into down payment on new investment property

a total of $8,000.00. Now, you are in a position to collect another $10,000.00 of upfront payments plus the monthly cash flow on two new homes. Remember, you didn't need to take money out of your pocket to buy these two new single-family homes. This is what I refer to as houses buying houses.

Houses Buying Houses

This is massive leverage. If each new home cash flowed at $300.00 a month, you would be doubling your cash flow without investing another penny out of your pocket. In addition, you would have two new homes with locked in profit of $25,000.00 each. The best investors I know get their money back from their investments as quickly as possible. Once they have recouped their original investment, they have nothing remaining at risk.

Their money can be reinvested, compounding their overall returns at astonishing rates. In most of the investments that my Income For Life System members make, they have their entire investments back within the first 12 months.

I teach my Income For Life System members to make money multiply consistently, constantly, and at will. If you had invested in the deal above, you would have invested $8,200.00 out of your pocket. You would have received a check for $9,000.00 shortly after you closed on the property. Use the $9,000.00 received as a down payment on another nice home. In essence, multiply money. This is an extremely powerful skill for you to learn and apply.

Let's take this just a little bit further to show you how powerful houses buying houses could be for you. Let's assume that you purchase three nice single-family homes and sell them on two-year Rent To Own programs. Figure 6 shows what your real estate portfolio would look like at the end of year three if you use your houses to buy houses.

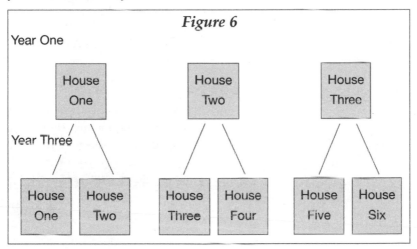

Figure 6

Three homes became six homes without any additional money invested out of your pocket. The proceeds from the sale of the homes purchased in year one covered the down payments on the 6 new homes purchased. The 6 homes purchased in year three would turn to 12 homes in year 5. The 12 homes purchased in year five would turn into 24 homes in year 7. This is an incredible wealth building machine!

This massive Income For Life System machine could be started with three 5% down payments on only three homes. In fact, Joe Mercadante, mentioned above, purchased 20 homes. He collected a total of $61,300.00 in upfront payments, created a monthly cash flow of $4,363.00, and has buyout profits locked in that total $580,442.00.

The Wealth-Building Secret

Let me wrap up by sharing a wealth-building secret. There are only two ways to get wealthy:

1. People working for you.
2. Money working for you.

People Working for You

Think about having 24 Rent To Own buyers that go to work each day to send you a large monthly rent check. Joe Mercadante has 20 Rent To Own buyers that go to work for him every day. He could be surfing in Hawaii, and 20 people are going to work to send him a check. The second part of the wealth secret is to have your money at work for you.

Money Working for You

In my earlier example, you will own 24 homes in 7 years. If you paid $120,000.00 for each home, you would own real estate worth $2,880,000.00. If homes are appreciating at just 5% a year, your equity in these homes increases by $144,000.00 each and every year. Your real estate is a powerful growing asset base that automatically builds wealth for you each and every year.

Clearly, the Income For Life System captures both of these aspects. True financial leverage is awarded to those who have people and money working for them at the same time. Once the first step is taken and the machine is set in motion, the wealth building begins. As wealth grows, we are lead to financial freedom and ultimately true independence. It all starts with one small step!

Anywhere in America

My Income For Life System has been so successful and is so formulaic that I have been training and exclusively licensing one real estate professional per city or area to work with investors, so there is probably someone in your area to help you. Or, if you happen to be a real estate agent, you might want to investigate this opportunity, if your area is still available. I assure you, working with a small group of investors who each buy 2 to 10 houses a year is a far better, more pleasant, more enjoyable business than listing and selling houses one at a time, only once to each client!

The Wealth Principle

Dan Kennedy teaches us to extract the Principle from situations we observe and to base our entrepreneurial activities on solid Principles. The Principle here in the Income For Life System for the investors and in the business system I provide to real estate agents is the same: *Don't* invent, use a proven "vehicle" differently. This is innovation, not invention.

Visit www.QuitWorkSomeDay.com to learn more about my Income For Life System and programs. You can contact my office at (440) 918-0047 or via fax at (440) 918-0347.

"Former Iowa Prison Guard Discovers...."
The Wealth Secret Hidden in Plain Sight in America's Heartland
Darin Garman

If you've seen my frequent ads in Forbes, Investors Business *Daily,* and other financial publications, you've seen the "Former Iowa Prison Guard" headline and maybe read my whole story. In brief, I was working in a dead-end job as a prison guard, frustrated, unhappy, barely paying the bills, and very worried about my family's future when, to add insult to angst, I was called on the carpet for something I hadn't done. I was cooling my heels in the waiting area outside the warden's office when I saw a beat-up copy of the book *Think and Grow Rich* on his bookshelf. I sat there and read the book. And it motivated me to quit my job—with no idea of what I was going to do!

Next, a discussion with a good friend led me to commercial real estate. I got licensed and began selling apartment buildings where I live, in and around Cedar Rapids, Iowa. Today, I control over 70% of that market, and the majority of buyers and sellers rely on me to handle their transactions. I've become such an expert at analyzing apartment buildings as well as commercial properties like shopping centers and office complexes, I've been invited to speak at a number of the biggest investment conferences in America. That's an amazing enough story, but it gets even better.

When I explained the unusual ways I worked with investors and the little-known virtues of investing specifically in "heartland of America" apartment buildings and commercial properties to Dan Kennedy, he said I had a "best kept secret" and should be sharing it with investors beyond the confines of Iowa or the Midwest. At his urging, I began running those ads I mentioned, and now I have a large, fast-growing club of sorts: small, large, and even multi-multimillionaire investors from New York to California, even overseas, who are investing with me in the heartland states.

Why would someone who lives and has his business in Los Angeles, Denver, Dallas, New York City, or Boston want to own real estate in Iowa? Actually, there are so many good reasons I can't list them all here. Two of the biggest have to do with the predictability and the stability of the market, compared to very volatile and much riskier areas, and, second, the exceptional opportunity to take tax advantaged cash income out of these investments as well as enjoying appreciation. A third reason is me, my expertise, my track record, and my conservative approach.

The Wealth Principle at Work

For me, it is not following the masses. I've learned, throughout my career, the wisdom of doing things differently than the majority. Everything about the way I do business is dramatically different from typical commercial real estate agents. In fact, I view that as only the "vehicle" I use. To most of my investor clients, I am in the wealth development business. We primarily use heartland of America investing as the vehicle, but we are working together to develop wealth. I'm not just selling properties. I am finding the right properties and structuring the best investments to meet my clients' objectives. Some clients want a lot of current income; others want deferred income. Some are sophisticated investors involved with things like 1031 exchanges. Other entrepreneurs want a simple, reasonably secure way to put part of their IRA, SEP, or Keough dollars to work at much higher yields than CDs, money market accounts, or similar investments.

I suggest the same "don't follow the masses" concept to you and to all other entrepreneurs and investors. For example, a lot of people, especially busy entrepreneurs, avoid real estate and invest in low yield CDs and money market accounts, invest in the stock market but with insufficient know-how and time to do well, or turn their money over to a money manager who often delivers disappointing results. As example, a friend of mine has had $500,000.00 under management, mostly in the stock market, with one of the top-ranked money managers, and in the past 5 years has had his portfolio lose as much as 14% of its value and then recover to base value plus 3%. In that same period, most of the real estate we've invested in has produced annual cash yields combined with appreciation of 10% to 16%. That's not to say you shouldn't invest in the market or have some of your money in the ultra-conservative CDs. But it is to say that you lose a lot by ignoring the investment preferred by most really wealthy people: commercial real estate.

Of course, you may not be willing to buy a one- to three- to five-million dollar apartment building by yourself. I've removed that obstacle.

Now the Best Kept Secret Is Readily Accessible to You

You are probably familiar with mutual funds. A mutual fund pools together people's money to buy hundreds and hundreds of stocks all at the same time. The benefit is a professional manager running the fund, making sure the pool of money is in the right investments, with no management on the part of the investor (it's done for you, the managers of the fund do it), spread risks, and a higher return (you hope).

The result is usually a decent return, say around 7%–10% on average, and a capital gains tax you need to pay once you sell your shares in the mutual fund. Of course, some funds focus on certain niches, and some funds are tax free like tax-free bond funds.

But, what if I told you of an investment with all of the same kind of attributes of a good mutual fund, BUT YOU COULD PREDICTABLY DOUBLE THE RETURN? Would that interest you? What if I could show you a way to invest your money, having it working overtime for you, professionally managed, giving you great tax savings (yep, you even save money on income taxes), AND you do not have to pay capital gains taxes when you sell—leaving Uncle Sam out of it!

In a nutshell, a large return, good monthly cash flow, zero capital gains taxes, AND no management on your part.

Do I have your attention yet? I hope so.

What I am going to show you will give you the real world ability to grow your wealth exponentially. It's like three or four investments wrapped up in one—all working together at the same time. Let me give you an example.

Let's say I buy 100 shares of ABC Mutual Fund at $1.00 per share. So, I have $100.00 invested into ABC Mutual Fund: $1.00 times 100 shares owned. Five years later, if the market was good, let's say that my $1.00 per share is now worth $1.50 per share. My $100.00 investment is now worth $150.00. I have made a 50% return on my money over the 5 years or a 10% annual return. Not too bad.

Now, if I sell, I will obviously profit and have to pay capital gains taxes to Uncle Sam, not to mention some state taxes as well (depending where you live). So, all that really happened here is that my investment appreciated and I paid capital gains taxes when it sold. This is purely an appreciation and capital gains type of investment. My overall return will, in this example, after I pay taxes, be even less than 10% because I have to pay capital gains taxes once I sell shares in this fund.

The problem is most investments are just like this in one way or another. You invest, profit a little, let your account increase a little, sell, and pay taxes.

Now, let's look at this mutual fund like you would my kind of investment—a pool of quality "heartland" commercial investment real estate property.

I put the same amount of money ($100.00) in the ABC Commercial Property Investment Fund AND I finance part of it, too. So, let's say I put $100.00 into the fund but borrow another $100.00. So, I have purchased 200 shares of ABC Commercial Property Investment Fund (200 times $1.00 per share), but I still have only $100.00 of my own money in it because the other $100.00 was borrowed.

I now control double the shares, 200, with the same amount of money out of my pocket, $100.00. Remember the other $100.00 is the bank's money, not mine.

So now I own twice the fund shares for the same investment out of pocket.

Now, let's say while I own this stock, it appreciates at the same rate as before, 10% per annum for five years. In five years, ABC Commercial Property Investment Fund is worth $1.50 per share.

But over the five years, let's say that ABC Commercial Property Investment Fund had so much cash flow coming to me monthly that I was also capable of paying back the $100.00 I borrowed. So, not only is my fund appreciating and paying me cash flow—at the same time it is also paying off my additional $100.00 of debt I used to buy more stock.

On top of that, when I file my tax return, Uncle Sam is going to give me some nice large tax breaks for owning ABC Commercial Property Investment Fund. These tax breaks will reduce the income generated by ABC. Even though I am profiting every year from ABC Fund in the form of nice monthly cash flow checks, I can use legal tax saving strategies to show a loss from ABC. The good news is that I can do this even though it made money year after year.

Lastly, when it comes time to sell my interest in ABC, Uncle Sam decides to give me a break. He tells me that when I sell ABC

I do not have to pay any capital gains taxes. I can sell, keep my profit, and legally defer any capital gains taxes.

Also remember, after all of this I have a pretty predictable income stream coming in month after month, no management, an exponential rate of return if I choose no capital gains taxes, AND I own double the shares.

Now, which investment would you take if you had to choose? I hope it's obvious.

That is how commercial investment real estate works in my world. When investors pool their money with me to purchase good commercial investment property, it blows away most other investments. See Figure 1. I hope my stock analogy brings this home for you. Can you see how this type of investment can exponentially grow your wealth vs. the traditional way?

Most people reading this book have probably heard of or have a friend involved in owning some type of investment real estate. If you are one that has never been an investment real estate owner, it is probably because of:

1. Your age or family status.
2. Your lack of knowledge that makes you uncomfortable about owning and investing in commercial real estate. You do not really totally understand the great benefits along with the cash flow you would receive. So, you put it off.
3. Lack of time. This is the biggie. Not enough time to really sit down, research, and educate yourself about the possibilities of commercial investment real estate.
4. You think it may be risky.
5. Maybe you haven't had that much interest until now.
6. You think other investments are much better (stocks, bonds, single-family homes, etc.)

Figure 1

A Typical Commercial Real Estate Investment Property

120 S. 12th St. Apartments

1. Purchase price paid: $750,000.00.

2. Investment: $150,000.00

3. Financed by lender: $600,000.00

4. Monthly payments to lender:
   $4,473.00 per month X 12 =
   $53,681 per year

5. Income from property: $125,000.00

6. Expenses: $48,000.00

7. Net income from property: $77,000.00

8. Cash flow:
   $77,000.00 Net income
   $53,681.00 Less annual financing
   $23,319.00 Annual cash flow

9. Cash return on $150,000.00:
   $23,319.00 ÷ $150,000.00 = 15%

10. Principal loan reduction (paid by
    tenants): $7,222.00

11. Appreciation: 2% or $15,000.00
    Total return
    $ 23,318.00 Cash flow
    +$ 7,222.00 Principal reduction
    +$ 15,000.00 Appreciation
    $ 45,540.00 Total cash flow or a
    30.36% Total cash flow/return

For good apartment or commercial property analysis software that is easy to use go to www.commercial-investments.com.

Well, the process of being an owner, a profitable owner, mind you, can be an easy and hassle-free experience when you work with me or someone like me. There is really no need to let any of these obstacles get in your way. For example, my customers and clients are surprised at how easy it is working with me and how much is really done for them. The best part is getting all of the benefits of great investment real estate without having to commit to being a commercial investment real estate expert. The leverage of time and money here is huge. But, you still get all of the same benefits of owning the property as if you were there managing the property day in and day out! The property is working for you while you sleep, while you are working, or while you are goofing off—and throwing off great cash flow and tax savings, and appreciating all at once. What else is better than that?

This is why one of the best kept investment secrets out there today is the PRIVATE INVESTMENT REAL ESTATE FUND.

By being involved in a private fund, you literally have your cake and eat it, too. Not only do you have a great investment working overtime for you and giving you quantum results, you also have an expert overseeing the fund and properties with no personal time of yours in it at all! You literally become an

Active Owner of Great Cash Flow Investment Real Estate While Not Being Active in the Day-to-Day Management Functions, Etc. You simply get a cash flow check once a month (if that is what you like) and a report detailing what happened in the prior month.

Actually, for some investors, there is something even better than that!

In many cases, I work with investors who prefer outright ownership of their own property or properties, with management provided, so it's "hands off." Others prefer joining one or several other investors with me in owning a particular property. However, many people are still uncomfortable with actually owning all or part of an apartment building or commercial property, especially in a distant location, especially when they are required to sign for a lot of the debt personally. This stops them from participating. But, after an enormous amount of work, I've developed the perfect solution: an actual private real estate investment fund that works just like the mutual fund you looked at for example purposes earlier. One of the best kept secrets in the entire financial world is this kind of professionally managed, private real estate fund. As an investor in such a fund, you get all the same benefits as an investor would with a single property, like the 120 S. 12th Street Apartments example, but you have your risk spread over a group of properties and you are not liable for any debt!

By being involved in this type of innovative fund, you literally can have your cake and eat it too! You become an active owner of great real estate investments, with the cash flow and tax benefits of active ownership, yet you still have no involvement in day-to-day property management and no debt liability. You get a check and a report every month.

In *Think and Grow Rich*, Napoleon Hill gave a number of examples of entrepreneurs who literally changed the way a particular business or industry functioned. The one that sticks in my mind is the store clerk who "invented" the self-serve supermarket. Prior to his invention, customers had to tell a clerk what they wanted, then wait around while he fetched the products. The self-serve supermarket concept opened the door to far greater variety of products, a kind of privacy for the shopper—you can take whatever time you like reading labels, comparing prices, and choosing what you want—and lower prices. His idea revolutionized the way people shop and the way the retail industry operates, all for the better. I've followed that example in rethinking the way people can invest in real estate to preserve all the benefits for the investor yet remove all the drawbacks and obstacles that block most people from those benefits!

$$\odot \quad \odot \quad \odot$$

For more information about Darin Garman, these types of investments, heartland of America properties, and private funds, visit www.commercial-investments.com or call (800) 471-0856, and enter an access code: #4002.

"Crisis Investing":
Amazing Opportunities in
PRE-Foreclosure Real Estate
Jeff Kaller

N apoleon Hill wrote, "In every adversity lies the seed of equal or greater opportunity." When a person or family gets into such financial trouble that they cannot meet their home mortgage payments, there's opportunity in their adversity to help them and to profit enormously—before the "foreclosure wolf" arrives at the door. That's what I want to talk to you about in this chapter. Also, there's a high probability of a fore-closure crisis, a huge tidal wave of foreclosures, in the very near future, and for savvy investors, that, too, represents opportunity.

Just eight short years ago, I was a struggling, disgruntled chef, building someone else's dreams, working tons of hours with no real game plan to change my situation. My newborn daughter, Allie, spent her first year growing up with a dad who was always working and never around. My wife, Sofia, and I loved each other but were always in heated, never-ending conversations about money or should I say, the lack of it. Even my two dogs, Gypsy and Daisy, would growl at me once I dragged myself home after five days of double shifts at the restaurant. I worked hard to get ahead, until I realized unless I made a change, I'd end up just another "schmo" working hard and not smart. So, one late night, in front of the boob tube, while I drowned my sorrows in a Bacardi rum and Coke and watched a late night guy talk about how to make money investing in real estate, I took a leap of faith, despite the negative cynicism from my wife, friends, and co-workers.

Just 24 months later, I had amassed millions in equity, owning more than 50 rental properties. Sadly, my vision of owning 300 free and clear properties was destroyed by lack of cash flow. I had bought these properties all wrong! It took me two years to clean up this mess, even losing a house to foreclosure. During this process, I recognized the power of dealing with properties behind on payments, and to-date, I have shown others these proprietary techniques, allowing others to produce more usable cash now, today, than any other niche in real estate.

For the last six years, I've created an entire team focused on buying defaulted homes and partnering with countless others to do the same. My companies have taught thousands of students with no previous real estate business to make millions. I'm the guy everybody goes to when they want to learn debt negotiation and investing in pre-foreclosure properties.

Why the Timing Is Ideal for My Approach to *Accelerated* Wealth via Foreclosure and Pre-Foreclosure Real Estate

There is an impending disaster banks have gotten themselves into and, in part, been forced into. Their problems are our opportunities.

All lenders, banks, and financial institutions have an acceptable tolerance level of properties that enter into a default status once homeowners get behind on their house payments. These ratios are very publicized and must be provided to stockholders who, as a combined group, carry enormous control on publicly held companies. Many such publicly held companies in this country are way beyond acceptable levels of loans in default. This is fact, not opinion. To remain solvent, these same lenders have done the unthinkable:

> *Instead of correcting these defaulted loans, lenders have created new loan programs, usually carrying much more risk, to loan out more money. This increases the performing side of the equation while generating additional revenue through underwriting fees, loan points, prepayment penalties, etc. The ploy is simply to out run delinquent ratios without ever fixing what's broke!*

Guess who's there to help rid these lenders of the nonperforming assets? People like me. As pre-foreclosure investors, our job is to contact these troubled homeowners and help them *prior* to their property being foreclosed on by the bank. We can do this three ways: helping the lender to enable the seller to enter a "work-out plan" or repayment plan for the arrears (if successful, we can charge a fee), taking over the seller's loan and becoming the new owner without transferring the loan liability to us, or negotiating a short sale whereby the lender accepts less than what is owed as a payoff in lieu of repossessing the property and having to resell it. We help the homeowner AND improve a lender's overall numbers. Once we resell the property, a major profit is made.

In a way, it is like having three businesses in one.

By the way, this is done by controlling the property without any of our own money OR credit.

The Right Opportunity for the Serious, Sophisticated Entrepreneur

Although I have frequently taken people with no real estate or business experience and taught them how to make very large profits and create wealth on pre-foreclosure real estate, this opportunity is admittedly not for everybody. It is, in my opinion, for the very serious entrepreneur, willing to invest a reasonable amount of time and effort learning a new and very lucrative business. It is a business to be actively involved in, part-time or full-time.

Ill-Advised New Laws Will Actually Make the Crisis Worse—and Give Us Even Greater Opportunity

Despite all the other challenges these poor homeowners face once in default, the worst is yet to come. Some states have passed laws to protect homeowners from unscrupulous investors trying to take advantage of them and their equity. Just as in any industry, there are always those looking to make a quick buck at the expense of others. Ironically enough, those of us who are ethical and fair stand to make more than those who are not.

Some state lawmakers are proposing bills that, if passed, would prohibit anyone from contacting a seller who is three months behind on his payments. This is scary. Imagine a poor homeowner who doesn't know which way to turn for help. Remember, I used to be one of those people because I lost my house to foreclosure. What about a new lender who might otherwise refinance this poor customer and help save his home?

In some areas, realtors can't contact a homeowner to help them to sell. Even an attorney who could possibly help the homeowner through protective bankruptcy laws cannot approach them. Crazy as it may seem, but more interesting, some states have created exemptions allowing realtors and attorneys to contact the homeowners while all other people in our free enterprise system are forbidden. How do these policies affect you, me, and other legitimate investors?

First, very, very few states have actually passed these laws, but you can imagine how drastically the foreclosure rates will increase when these unfortunate laws constructed to help the homeowners actually hurt them. Although some banks will go out of business, unregulated, savvy, and ethical pre-foreclosure investors will thrive. Through hard work and extensive research, our team has cracked the code and will continue to operate in an effort to help keep sellers from losing their homes and/or all their equity. We will also continue to help lenders dispose of unwanted properties instead of having to foreclose.

An Antiquated System Lenders Face When Disposing of Unwanted Properties

Once a homeowner gets three months behind on house payments, the lender will perform an equity analysis to project the possible loss that could be incurred if they have to foreclose on a homeowner and take the property back. This entire process is called a short sale and is processed through their loss mitigation department. Within each department are debt negotiators called loss mitigators. These are the individuals we communicate with when we are working with a homeowner on a potential short sale.

Unfortunately, all lenders and loss mitigation departments are swamped processing these short sale requests because of the sheer number of homes in default, as I have already discussed. Each mitigator typically handles 100 files each month, and over half could be processed if they had a chance!

It's this antiquated system in the short sale system that is bad for the banks and tough on the average investor. However, where there is a challenge, there also lies some entrepreneur out there who has learned how to work effectively in an environment that seems to confuse everyone else.

In summary, this entire pre-foreclosure industry is truly poised to explode! The writing isn't just on the wall, it is splattered across buildings and single-family houses all across our great country. The timing has never been better to be in this field.

I'm in the business of helping by providing positive solutions in otherwise dismal and chaotic situations. Our team gets paid handsomely; our students make more money than they have ever dreamed of. We are willing to support a limited number of entrepreneurs getting started in this business each month. We provide comprehensive start-up training and continuing assistance. We even step in and literally negotiate the short sale deals you find in your area!

Are There Secrets?

Dan Kennedy likes a quote from Aristotle Onassis, "Wealth comes from knowing what others do not know." I have found paths to wealth for myself and my students by uncovering knowledge, information, and opportunities that the vast majority of entrepreneurs and investors are either completely unaware of or ignore because of their apparent complexity. The relatively complex nature of the pre-foreclosure business dampens competition, and that's a good thing!

For more information, visit www.mrpreforeclosure.com/ studentdeals or call (800) 646-2574 to receive your free information package and a two-hour DVD, "How to Cash in on Short Sales with Half the Work."

The Secret to
Entrepreneurial Wealth
Stephen Oliver

oo many years ago now, I was finishing up a degree in International Economics at Georgetown University, on the way to my cherished MBA at Harvard, Stanford, or Wharton, with every expectation of a long career in big corporate America.

I was working my way through school as a martial arts instructor and branch manager for arguably the only professional business organization running martial arts schools at that time. As I closed in on graduation, I put together my resume and interviewed with the likely candidates for employment. I planned on working for a couple of years before returning to business school.

After talking to Chase, Proctor & Gamble, IBM, and SUNY, I had a remarkable revelation: my existing profession was not only more fun and more significant, but potentially more lucrative than any of those corporate options.

Through a radical leap of faith, I camped out at the Library of Congress, the SBA, and SCORE and studied everything I could get my hands on about sales, advertising, and direct response marketing. I then put together my business plan (thinking erroneously that some wise banker would fund me) and in a rented U-Haul moved from Washington, DC, to Denver, Colorado.

Then I launched my business—with little more than a $10,000.00 loan from my parents and a pocket full of credit cards. I built a $1,000,000.00 martial arts school business with 1,500 active students across 5 locations in about 18 months. All the while the support I was receiving from most friends and associates went something like this: "Yeah, 'play karate' for a couple of years then you can get a real job."

While still in Washington, DC, I made a transition that few make. I went from athlete (or technician) to teacher. Then, as I decided to really make my chosen art into a career, I continued the transition rather quickly (at 21 years old) of moving from teacher to salesman to marketer. In retrospect, my early success was almost completely due to recognizing that it was most important for me to become an excellent marketer of martial arts lessons and least important to be a "master of the martial arts."

Once in Denver, I made the next necessary transition. I moved from excellent teacher, salesperson, and marketer to teacher again. This time to teacher of marketing, sales, and teaching skills to staff and associates in order to replicate myself across multiple locations.

I now dominate an industry that is populated mostly by athletes—and occasionally a quality teacher. Only rarely in my budding industry does someone like myself come along and realize that all businesses succeed or die on effective marketing systems. In the case of a multiunit retail or service business, that success depends upon scalability and the ability to replicate successful marketing systems across the organization.

Twenty-three years later, my role has morphed again, in a way that I believe really maximizes my talents and gives me an opportunity to not only be a "Martial Arts Millionaire" but in a way that allows me now to develop many other "Martial Arts Millionaires."

My most recent role has two components. The first is that of coach and consultant to martial arts schools throughout the United States and Canada and to organizations as far a way as Bahrain, Europe, South Africa, and Australia. The second is that of mentor to others replicating my school structure on a single unit and in a citywide or statewide master franchise.

It's this second role that I am most excited about and where the opportunity is greatest to grow many more millionaires by sharing what I've spent millions of dollars and over 30 years developing.

Before I go any further, let me point out a couple of imbedded lessons for anyone who owns a business or who is planning on going into business.

First, for most it's vitally important to mentally and physically move away from being the doer of the activity of your business as rapidly as possible. In the vast majority of the cases, the role of doing the activity of your business, whether it be martial arts instruction, painting, dry cleaning, serving food, or repairing or programming computers, is the easiest to replace, provides the lowest compensation, and restricts your personal growth and that of your business.

Other school owners and other business people often assume that the key factor in growing my business is having a "martial arts expert" at each location. I can tell you that many years later the teachers are the easiest employees to find and the least expensive to hire. Years ago, I developed systems that systematically produce quality martial arts teachers both through six-week intensive "quick-start" programs and through systematic cultivation from our population of thousands of martial arts students (our customers). A far more valuable employee is the one who can "sell" our product, not the technician. The sales role is taught, and the expert sales persons (I call them program directors) are trained through scripted and organized procedures.

In fact, as I grow my business, I am NOT looking for people who have martial arts skills. I can hire and train that role too easily. I am looking for individuals focused on growing a "sales and marketing" business who are capable of and willing to train others to support customer service, sales, and marketing roles. My organization is operating in an industry with few viable competitors, huge public interest, and incredible untapped opportunity, available to any qualified individual who is ready to impact a huge number of families and earn a great living in the process.

Second, as a business owner, your most highly compensated role is the ability to lead, inspire, and teach others to complete the day-to-day operations of your business. Even the best technical person encounters a disappointingly low ceiling to his or her income. The most gifted salesperson (unless selling Gulfstream jets or multimillion dollar contracts) quickly finds a ceiling to his or her own income. It's the person who can implement systems that can be taught to many and inspire them to high accomplishment whose income has an unlimited ceiling.

Third, an early discovery for me was finding the right market and designing our service to that market. Many of my friends and competitors in the martial arts field lament the poor quality of clientele they attract. I have no such complaint. Before opening my first business I undertook extensive demographic market research to make sure I located where there were lots of families with money and with a predisposition for my service. Soon after, I discovered that the family and children's market was a much better market for me than the traditional 18- to 35-year-old group that most others taught. My discoveries that families with good incomes would pay well for success training and character development for their kids, and that their willingness to pay a premium price for our service survived up and down economies and individual ups and downs added millions to my income over the years. I often charge double, triple, or quadruple what other schools charge while teaching higher quality clients who stay with me much longer.

Finally, a path that I didn't take but which I'm thoroughly convinced would have saved me ten or more years of trial and error: franchising. Although the opportunity was not available to me in the martial arts industry when I started in 1983, it certainly is today. If I had had the choice, I would have taken the franchising route rather than striking out completely on my own. All franchise organizations provide the opportunity to be "in business for yourself, but not by yourself," and in our case, my company provides the most extensive support structure as I've seen in any franchise business. A great benefit of running one of our martial arts schools is having the ability to combine a fun environment, relatively low capital requirements, and excellent income potential with a truly valuable service developing leaders and individuals of high character.

The many systems and processes that I've perfected in my Mile High Karate schools came from extensive trial and error. Occasionally I got it right the first time; much more frequently, I cycled through 5, 7, or 11 experiments before finding the right key to make a system work. Everything from step-by-step sales systems to staff training and development processes have been diligently developed through my own trial and error and by modeling success stories throughout the world.

At Mile High Karate, I have developed an incredibly effective curriculum that teaches kids and families discipline and confidence. It creates character and imbues "Indomitable Spirit." Additionally, I've perfected step-by-step selling processes that move families from "suspects" to "prospects" to "new students" to "Black Belt candidates" and ultimately to Black Belts and leaders. I've developed powerful, and in many areas, automated marketing systems that bring in new students and prepare them for my "back-end" upgrades. And finally, I've developed a training school and process that can ramp up new staff quickly and develop a quality team to run many locations.

Who am I looking for to grow my organization? Men and women who are excited about growing a service business. Those who will follow proven systems step-by-step to success. Individuals who for a single location can bring $75,000.00 to $100,000.00 to invest in their new business start-ups or who can invest a higher level of investment and management talent into a

"Master Franchise" relationship in a city or region. I am NOT looking specifically for individuals with martial arts talent or background. An enthusiasm for working with kids and adults and a willingness to manage sales and marketing systems are essential.

The Wealth Principle

Oddly, Dan did not specifically address the power of system in this book, but he certainly teaches it to those of us in his coaching groups and his clients. Even though I am in what many consider an unusual business, it is as much about system as is McDonalds. With each passing year, I am increasingly aware of the fact that most entrepreneurs operate by the seat of their pants, without well-thought-out, proven, step-by-step systems for every aspect of their businesses. I believe the amount of wealth you are able to accumulate as an entrepreneur is directly linked to how systemized your business is—so you are free to focus on big things, not trivia.

Stephen Oliver is the author of several books for his industry, including Direct Response Marketing for Martial Arts Schools *as well as* Everything I Wish I Knew When I Was 22. *He is a 7th Degree Black Belt in Tae Kwon Do, honor's graduate of Georgetown University, and earned his MBA from the University of Denver. He provides business training and coaching to martial arts school owners and teachers and is*

franchising his Mile High Karate concept throughout North America by converting existing schools and by bringing new entrepreneurs and investors into the industry. To learn more, visit www.MileHighFranchise.com or call (800) 795-2695.

Unusual Investing
Strategies Pay Off
Jerry A. Jones

From about age 7, I told my parents regularly that I had two goals in life: "I'm going to be a millionaire, and I'm going to be president of my own company." Fortunately, they told me, "You can do whatever you set your mind to." The best part was they actually meant it.

By age 28, I'd knocked out both goals. (I tried to get there sooner but had a few crashes and burns along the way.)

I grew up the all-American kid in a small town in southwest Washington. My parents were and are completely salt-of-the-earth, hard-working, ethical people. I have one older brother who constantly pushed me. And for many years, I followed in his footsteps because I liked his choices and I saw his successes and wanted them as well. Later, I would recognize this as an important principle—that of emulating what works well for those whose shoes you'd maybe like to fill.

Let me give you some brief background.

At age 10, I started the proverbial neighborhood lawn mowing business. I quickly made a deal with the neighbor to get her rider mower from her so I could take on more accounts and get them done quicker. I learned early the value of "no money down transactions" and trading sweat-equity for something I wanted but didn't have the cash to purchase. Ten quick lawn trims later and it was all mine, along with a junked-out push mower that burned more oil than gas. I appreciate now the fact my parents didn't ante up the $100.00 it cost me in lawn trims to equip my new landscaping business.

Just a year or so later, *while continuing to trim lawns*, I took a far less labor intensive job at a baseball batting cage and pro shop. I earned a whopping $3.15 an hour, watched a lot of M*A*S*H reruns, finished my homework every day, and got *very* good at hitting an 80 mph fastball. I was experiencing an early double income. I found I was the richest preteen and later richest teenager I knew, and I really enjoyed the feeling.

Today, my life is enjoyable and still very rich in many ways. I find I have to put my back against the wall to create my own brand of stress, otherwise I quickly bore.

I also have this penchant for doing the unusual and what most would think impossible. I find it pays extremely well because most would never dream of taking it on.

My regular income today (and the first million I made) is from my business that serves dentists, helping them attract more patients and keep those they already have. Over the last few years, I've sold over $10 million dollars of goods and services to them, *yet I'm not a dentist*. I even closely advise a group of about 50 dentists in a mastermind group (www.PersonalDentalCoach.com) on an ongoing basis, each paying in excess of $8,000.00 in yearly dues.

Early on, I recognized a very important trend in the dental industry. The services we provided to dentists at that time were provided in bulk fashion, meaning a dentist would first purchase envelopes, special stationery, and a magazine from my company and then have their employees (we call them a "team" in the industry) assemble, print, and mail the whole package, which was essentially a practice "newsletter."

After a few years, I realized there was a resistance developing among our clients. They wanted the results of doing a newsletter—referrals, education, patient retention, and so on—but they didn't want their highly paid team (and rightfully so) engaged in the act of putting it all together.

This big discovery led to very important changes in not just my core business, but in the thinking I've applied to every business I've started since.

This trend of wanting "results" without doing anything has become huge. My breakthrough has opened doors for many entrepreneurs like myself who used to provide how-to information and now provide turn-key, "done-for-them" services to their clients. My friends and colleagues and fellow Dan Kennedy Platinum Inner Circle members Rory Fatt of Restaurant Marketing Systems and Ron Ipach of CinRon Marketing are two that immediately come to mind.

And, the benefits to clients are tremendous—their marketing gets done, their clients hear from them, they reap the financial and intrinsic rewards of referrals, education, retention, etc.

This big idea of "doing it for them" later reared its head as I began to develop other facets of my businesses and was actually instrumental in another breakthrough: expanding from providing turn-key dental practice *marketing services* to providing—you guessed it—*turn-key dental practices*, ready-to-go for dentists wanting to practice dentistry without the traditional headaches of running a business!

My reasoning was simple. I have down pat what most dentists do not! I have the ability to generate new patients with ease, and I felt my ability to assemble and manage a team of dental employees was well-suited for the task. Further, I felt it would lend a ton of credibility to my core business if I was actually intimately involved with the management side of a dental practice. (It's against the law to be involved in anything but that if you are not a licensed dentist.) So, I went out and raised about $200,000.00 in capital and hit the ground running. (Notice I didn't use my own cash for this! OPM, Other People's Money, is better suited for projects like this.)

At the time of this writing, I'm routinely experiencing $40,000.00+ months in this new dental practice and I have doctors from all over the state of Oregon asking how they can join in and practice there. It's nice to be wanted!

In the last year, I've also partnered with a dentist and have provided him my expertise and services in generating new patients to the point where the practice was able to drop a public health plan that was killing their profits. Now they are experiencing multithousand dollar days, where before a $1,000 day was considered excellent. (Information on all of my turn-key services is available at www.JerryJonesDirect.com.)

In addition, I've provided one of my dental practice office managers to train and implement systems in this other practice, essentially increasing the value of this doctor's secondary practice in exchange for 33% ownership of the facility. A sweet deal for both of us!

The great news about dental practices is they can sell for a nice multiple of their "sales," so I am expecting a nice payday when I decide to cash in my chips. Or, maybe I'll go out and purchase 15 or 20 offices and do it on a large scale. I guess it all depends on how ambitious I want to get, right? Because another big idea I've learned is that keeping my eye on one "thing" or business is fairly easy. Keeping my eye on three is difficult. Keeping my eye on 15 or 20 is actually *easier* than monitoring and trying to run 3! The reason is that with 15 or 20, risk is spread around or amortized over the group, whereas with 2 or 3, problems are larger and affect management in a more intense fashion. It's really all about managing risk.

If you have any interest in being an instrumental player in the health care field on the *business* side, this is an excellent opportunity. Feel free to contact me for more information.

Most recently, I've started another project, which *intentionally* has limited life and a big, big, multimillion dollar payday plus other perks. It was, believe it or not, easy to start.

Even considering as well as I've done in the dental industry, I have yet to find anything as lucrative as real estate. I've invested in bare land, created investment partnerships, purchased a huge 9,000-sq. ft. restaurant, torn it down to create condos, and even purchased a nice marina. I just signed the contract on bare land I'd like to develop into apartments over on the Oregon coast. All with such little money out of my pocket, if I told you, you'd probably not believe me.

Real estate has been the single biggest wealth-building factor I've utilized. In 2005, I'll add close to $2.5 million in net worth to my portfolio—and the best part is, it's not high-risk real estate; it's all recession-proof type stuff. If you don't know how to buy a house or commercial property with little or no money out of your pocket, you're cheating yourself and your family. I learned everything I know from my good friend Ron LeGrand.

Another interesting trend in real estate has been the fad associated with "reservation" deposits.

Just recently I put up $2,500.00 to reserve an escrow number for a new condo-hotel development in Seaside, Oregon. Here's why that's a good idea if you get the opportunity, and especially if it's near water. With my $2,500.00 deposit, I'm able to:

1. get my $2,500.00 back, risk-free,
2. buy a condo when they are completed,
3. *transfer my RIGHT TO BUY* to another individual.

Realistically, I can sell my right to buy to someone for double, triple, or more than I paid for it! It's a beautiful thing. It essentially works like an "option to buy."

Watching trends, investing my *income* with the intention of building *wealth* is truly what the game of business allows me to do.

Every wealthy person I know uses his "day" job to generate income, to build his lifestyle to create wealth.

Unless you start wealthy (liquid equity, i.e., cash in the bank), this proven formula will deliver. Set your goal, reverse engineer it, experience it.

Jerry A. Jones is president and CEO of Jerry Jones Direct, a dental practice advertising and marketing firm, and SofTouch Family Dental Group, Inc., a dental practice management firm, all based in Salem, Oregon. His books, Practice Building Success, Volumes I & II *are available direct from the publisher at (800) 311-1390. You can reach Jerry via fax at (503) 371-1299.*

Is There a "Secret" Government-Secured 24% Interest Rate?

Ted Thomas

I've been helping people create wealth for 16 years. I've worked with some very successful entrepreneurs and successful investors, even financial industry professionals who were unaware of what I'm about to reveal to you—a unique, little-known investment that trumps everything else in existence when it comes to the convergence of high yield and security.

This investment is crisis proof. It is immune to ups and downs in the economy, war, stock market crashes, real estate bubble bursts, and corporate bankruptcies.

It is government secured. Not exactly like the federal government secures bank deposits and CDs, through the FDIC, but just about as rock solid, with a state or county government agency guaranteeing your checks. On top of that, it is double guaranteed because it is also secured by real estate.

It pays super high, locked-in-place interest rates. These interest rates beat any other interest bearing investment, even in boom times. You get 16%, 18%, even 24% interest rates. The interest rate locked in when you invest is mandated by law and cannot be changed. It cannot rise or fall with Alan Greenspan's health or the stock market. It cannot be changed by a banker or insurance company executive.

It is easy to buy yourself, with no brokers or broker commissions. I am not telling you about it to sell it to you. I can't. You buy it direct from state or county governments, in your area or in different parts of the country. And there are no "sneaky" fund management fees or other hidden costs or charges.

You can invest just about any amount. Start with as little as $500.00 or invest $50,000.00. Use self-directed IRA or pension funds if you like. You can also shop around for higher rates, or take a slightly lower rate to reduce your shopping time, as I'll explain. You are not restricted to the state you live in. As of this writing, Florida pays 18%, Iowa pays 24%, and Arizona 16%.

I swear under oath all this is true, and I offer $10,000.00 to anyone who can prove it is false.

As brief introduction, I once owned over 1,800 apartment buildings, office buildings, and residences in three states—and I took a beating, incidentally, during one of those times that interest rates soared unexpectedly. About ten years ago, I became interested in less risky, safer, easier investing. After a lot of investigation and work, I perfected an approach to investing in the investment world's most selfishly guarded secrets, tax lien certificates. Almost every bank, insurance company, and pension fund regularly invests in these safe, high-yield certificates, but they keep it to themselves. The banks prefer selling you low interest CDs. Super-wealthy individuals also regularly, quietly buy tax lien certificates. But the "little guy" has been kept in the dark. And if you ask most financial planners or brokers about them, they'll either be ignorant or talk you out of investing in them, claiming it's "too complicated." But remember, there's no way for a broker to earn commission selling these things!

Admittedly, there is a *slight* drawback. It does take a little bit of knowledge, time, and effort to select the certificates you want and to buy them. It's usually best to physically go to an auction to bid and buy them—and a couple times a year, I take groups of my students and clients to an auction. But you can buy them direct from the government agencies at their offices, and even in some cases over the internet.

How the Tax Lien Process Works

In hundreds and hundreds of counties, towns, and cities, local governments have millions owed to them in unpaid, overdue property taxes. These are past due taxes on homes, shopping centers, apartment buildings, and land. By law, these properties cannot be sold or transferred unless and until these back taxes, the interest, and penalties are all paid. To fund police, fire, hospitals, schools, etc., the governments create and sell tax lien certificates linked to these unpaid taxes and the property the taxes are owed on. They sell the lien certificates to private investors, like you and me. Each lien certificate is 100% secured by the real estate it is attached to, guaranteed to be collected by the government for you, and paid to you by the government. There is no question whatsoever of "if," only a question of "when."

To prod these delinquent tax payers, the governments charge sky-high interest rates and penalties, all of which go to you if you own the tax lien certificate!

Your Three Options as a
Tax Lien Investor—They're all Good

You can simply sit on the tax lien certificate you own and wait until the property owner wants to transfer or sell the property, decides to pay his back taxes (maybe to clean up his credit), or dies and the property has to transfer. When that happens, the government hands you a check for your investment amount plus all the accumulated interest and penalties. It may be years, or it may be only months.

Most of these certificates have a built-in "D-Day." On that date, if the property owner hasn't paid up, you can if you want to, pull the trigger, foreclose, and take the real estate. That means you get the entire house or building just for the price of the tax lien certificate. I can show you lots and lots of cases where my students have wound up with great houses, other buildings, acres and acres of land, for pennies on the dollar, and turned right around and sold them for huge profits. Just as example, one of my students, Chad Knox wound up with two houses in

Detroit, one from a $10,000.00 tax lien and foreclosure, the other from a $24,000.00 tax lien. He sold the first house for $65,000.00, the second for $55,000.00, for total profits of $86,000.00.

Or you can "flip" the certificate for a profit, especially as you get close to "D-Day." Real estate speculators eager to foreclose will often buy these certificates and pay you a handsome profit.

Real Investors, Real Money

If you invite me to send you a complete information package about my step-by-step tax lien investing system, I'll also send you a small mountain of proof, actual examples, from my students, including amounts paid for their Certificates, interest rates, length of time held, and profits. One of my most active students, Scott Shires of Denver, Colorado, has purchased more than 728 tax lien certificates, and 459 of them required investments of only $500.00 or less. His interest rates have averaged 22% to 27%.

Tax lien certificates are available in 39 states, so it's easy to invest. While on vacation in Texas, Cheryl Hyland, a Canadian, invested $7,390.00 in a tax lien certificate and only four months later it was paid off—she received $9,187.50 back. A $1,797.00 profit, a 25% gain in just 120 days. Hers is not an unusual example either. I'll be happy to show you hundreds.

Who Should Invest in Tax Lien Certificates?

Do you want to retire someday soon? If so, this is a great way to salt away money now that will pay you big future dividends. Or it's an interesting retirement activity. Do you need to set aside funds for a son's or daughter's college education? Buy the right tax lien certificates with the right "D-Days," and earn 16% to 24% interest. Do you have money that's asleep? Maybe IRA, SEP, Keough or other savings all parked in low interest CDs? Are you intrigued with everything you've read and heard about making money in real estate but have precious little time to play the game? You can "back in" by investing in these incredibly safe, secure tax lien certificates.

The Wealth Principle

I tell people: look beneath the surface. The best opportunities are usually not readily, obviously visible to everyone, or instantly and easily understood by every Tom, Dick, and Mary. In this case, you can settle for 3%, 4%, or 5% returns on your savings, or you can get 14%, 18%, or 24%. It's up to you. Your decision could be the difference between being "comfortable" or getting really rich. You work hard for your money. Shouldn't it work as hard as possible for you?

To receive a free information package about tax lien investing and complete home study manuals and courses, tele-classes, and even buying trips to auctions, fax a request to Ted Thomas at (321) 449-9938 or call (321) 449-9940 and ask for the offer from the No B.S. Wealth *book.*

How Entrepreneurs Can Use Mortgages to Fix Their Cash Flows, Take Full Advantage of the Tax Code, and Get Cash to Invest!
Scott Tucker

G randpa was wrong. The kind of advice that we got growing up, the stuff we heard "at the top of the stairs," as Dan puts it, the stuff we all too often hear from our friends—most, if not all of it, is wrong!

The days where you needed to put 20% down on a home purchase are gone, and so are the days where *all* debt is bad. While we all strive to be 100% debt-free, we all also know that *borrowing* can sometimes benefit us much more than waiting to have a 20% down payment or paying all cash for something.

Often, the borrower can benefit much more than the lender. But what the borrower must focus on is not how much the lender benefits, but how the borrower can take advantage of a great opportunity through borrowing. The opportunity must be rock solid and profitable to justify debt.

You're still a fool to bet the farm on a roulette wheel, but at least once a year all of us even if you've got your eyes shut and your ears plugged, come across at least *one* investment opportunity sure to succeed. Unless a comet strikes. And even then, maybe with the right insurance . . . .

About three years ago, I zapped all the equity from a condominium that was my principal residence. I took that money, and I put nearly $96,000.00 down on two commercial condos. (*Commercial* lenders do still require 20% down in most cases.) I bought these two commercial condos at preconstruction prices in a very hot and still developing area.

I needed one commercial condo for my then new mortgage brokerage business. The State of Illinois requires that I have a commercial office, not simply work from home. The other commercial condo I bought was as an investment.

I paid $480,000.00 for those commercial condos combined, $96,000.00 down, the rest financed over 30 years. Only 18 months after I closed on those condos, their value is about $660,000.00. I'm selling one, "vanilla boxed," pending sale next month at $317,500.00, and paying only 15% capital gains tax (thanks to President George W. Bush) on a gain of about $87,500.00. So, I made $74,375.00 after taxes, in about 18 months, doing nothing. Oh, and I've still got the other commercial condo, too! But I'm keeping that.

That's only one example of how using mortgages to *borrow* money can *make* you money. What if you don't have $96,000.00 of home equity? And you don't know how or where to invest in *commercial* real estate?

An answer can be found in this story of my customers, Matt and Janice Gunn. Matt owns Moonfly Inc., an advertising agency. By getting them a new mortgage—using my exceptionally productive methods—I was able to save them $2,156.98 every month on their monthly bills, improve their credit, pay off all three of their mortgages, their car loan, and 24 credit cards. I even got them $15,924.56 in cash left over at the closing to fund the IRAs, invest in residential or commercial real estate, or save tax-free for the kids' college, whatever they want to do with it.

They also got two months with nothing to pay on anything. That kept *another* $10,320.36 in their pockets right there, more money to save and/or invest.

Each of those 24 credit cards was still open for their use, and it was their decision which to keep, which to close.

I always recommend that my customers keep four credit cards open besides the conventional first mortgage that I get for them. This keeps their credit scores up. Not enough credit lines open on your credit report, and your score will sink. And you'll not be treated fairly later.

So they save $2,156.98 every month. That's $25,883.72 a year, tons of money they can save and invest. Over ten years, they can invest $259,000.00. It almost doesn't matter *what* they invest in, they'll be much further ahead by having re-arranged their debt and leveraged their equity. They could buy single-family homes, preconstruction condos, commercial properties, or, for that matter, invest well in stocks and bonds. They could follow the advice and use the methods in the other experts' Bonus Chapters in this book. By any reasonable method, this liberated cash for investments should make them millionaires.

Nearly all of my clients are also getting huge additional tax-deductions as a result of what I'm doing for them. Most now get to write-off 100% of the interest they now pay, as most of what I do involves their principal residence. (The interest on their credit card balances and most other debt was not tax deductible.) They may even get tax benefits on rental property.

Learn from Pascal Kerin, another customer of mine. He emigrated to the United States from Ireland a few years ago to make it big as a builder. He started from scratch, built one small three- or four-unit project at a time, and snowballed it to the next deal, and so on.

When Pascal called me for help, he was in a tight spot for cash to finish the rehab of the three-flat he lived in and to finish the construction of a new three-flat with his business partner. (A three-flat is a common structure here in Chicago that looks like a three-story house squared-off, with a flat roof, but is actually a three-unit apartment building.)

Pascal needed to raise some money to get these two projects finished.

Like many business owners, Pascal couldn't show tax returns to the lender. It wasn't that he doesn't pay his taxes, just that his tax returns wouldn't be of any use with the lender's underwriters. No pay stubs, no W-2s. Nothing "normal."

I got Pascal $59,820.40 in cash. I also got him two months without mortgage payments to make on the 3-flat that he owned and lived in. That freed-up *another* $5,526.84 right there. Over $65,000.00 cash, *borrowed* to *make* money.

And here's one that might pique your interest. My client Cheryl Sloane called me up and told me that she needed cash to start, of all things, a women's boutique selling lingerie and "other unmentionable items."

She had just been turned down by her life-long bank, and every other bank in town. No one wanted to lend her *any* money. I'm sure many entrepreneurs reading this can empathize!

I ended up getting her $82,865.43 in cash to start the business, plus two months with no payments due to anyone, except utilities and groceries. Those two months with no bills kept *another* $4,658.36 in her pocket to put into the business.

I not only got her all the cash she needed for "G Boutique," but I combined her two old mortgages and paid off every other bill she had. I even settled a collection against her for less than 60% of the balance due. That meant that we only had to pay the people at the collection agency $5,760.00, rather than the $9,600.61 that they had been hassling her about. So there's $3,840.61 saved right there. And the collection calls stopped, too.

All that cleaned up her credit report. And she only ended up having to pay $22.57 more a month! Over $85,000.00 in cash to start a new business for only $22.57 a month! Can't beat that.

I hope after reading all this that you can now understand what I meant about the all-too-often overlooked opportunities to *borrow* money, through mortgages, to *make* money. Money freed up, very quickly, to invest in many things: new businesses, new real estate properties, whatever you like.

Scott Tucker is a mortgage broker in Chicago, Illinois. He specializes in nonprime and different mortgage refinances. In

addition, Scott now helps folks, from working-class homeowners to affluent individuals, invest in "managed for 'em" commercial real estate properties, especially in cities other than where they reside. He is able to "shake loose" for them the cash with which to do this investing. He also provides seminars, coaching, and consulting for other mortgage brokers in the United States and Canada. Scott may be reached only via fax at (773) 327-2842.

How to Best Finance a College Education—and Save Tens of Thousands of Dollars

Ron Caruthers

There are multiple paths that must converge to get to wealth. There's the way you think, which Dan has written and spoken about extensively. There's the income you create but, more important, the percentage of that income you keep and multiply. One often overlooked path is the money you save from waste. Most busy entrepreneurs actually waste a lot of money. Because they are too busy to pay attention to different things, they just write the check and run faster to earn more. With some trivial expenses that's okay. But for something in the $60,000.00 and up range, like your son's or daughter's college education, that's a mistake. After all, to net $60,000.00 after taxes, you probably need at least $100,000.00 in income. If your business has 50% costs of goods and overhead, you need to sell $200,000.00 of whatever you sell. So ignoring opportunities to send your kids to college for free or nearly free is like flushing $200,000.00 or more down the toilet—per child! If you happen to have four or five kids, we're talking about a millionaire sum.

How to Finance a College Education

One of the biggest impediments to long term wealth accumulation is the little expenses that seem to add up and get in the way of true wealth. And for those of you who are parents, one of your biggest expenses of all will be your children.

From bringing them home as cute little babies (most often with a whopping hospital bill), through their younger years—with piano lessons, soccer camps, and braces—none of that really holds a candle to the cost of a college education.

If you haven't been following what schools cost these days, even the cheapest community college is several thousand dollars a year, and that does NOT include room and board.

In California, where I live and run my college planning practice, the cost of the cheapest state school, including room and board, is over $15,000.00 per year. And most students need more than four years to graduate. Private schools start at over $30,000.00 per year, with many costing as much as $45,000.00 per year. In other words, you'll be spending somewhere between $60,000.00 and $180,000.00 for *each* of your children to attend school.

And, if you finance that education through the traditional government-sponsored loans, you can be charged as much as ten points on the front end as an origination fee (in other words, they want an additional 10% to give you the money). This, plus the interest on your loan, can *double* the actual amount that you spend.

Even if you've only got one child, this can make a serious dent in your cash flow and wealth accumulation plans.

Well, it gets worse.

If you have young children, you can expect the cost of college to double in the next seven years. So, if your children are still in grade school, instead of $15,000.00 to $45,000.00 per year, you're looking at $30,000.00 to $90,000.00 per year, or $120,000.00 for a four-year state school education and $360,000.00 for a private school degree.

Is it worth it? Well, according to the US Census Bureau, college graduates with four-year degrees earn, on average, 70% more than those that just graduate with a high school diploma, so you could argue that it is. But still, that's a whole lot of money.

And no one really seems to have the answers about who *really* gets any aid or *how* to get it yourself.

Most people assume that they make too much money to qualify for any assistance. Or that their child needs to be an athlete, a straight A student, or a minority for the school to take an interest in them.

Worse, most guidance counselors usually aren't any help at all in the process. And, as I'll show in a minute, even the most well-intentioned CPA or financial planner often gives advice that hurts more often than it helps.

Depressed yet?

Don't be. In the last 11 years, I've cracked the code on how to make this an absolute breeze and how to get thousands of dollars, no matter how much money you make or how good a student you have. My methods have worked for over 1,125 individual families that I've personally worked with, including everyone from single moms to CEOs to a famous country singer.

So, here are the five things you must know to get started and get a boatload of FREE money:

Five Things You Must Know to Save Thousands on College

Step 1: You must know the rules that the Department of Education uses to determine "need based" aid.

Here's what this means. Congress has a formula that uses 74 different criteria from your family's situation to assess what they feel you can afford for your student each year—no matter how much that school costs.

They take into account things like your income and assets, your student's income and assets, how many in your family will be going to school that year, the age of the older parent, and on and on.

All this data is then run through a needs-analysis formula to calculate a magic number called an EFC, or Expected Family Contribution. (I teach classes on this all the time, and I'm still shocked at the number of parents with kids already in college who have *no clue* what an EFC is.)

This amount is then subtracted from the total cost of attendance of each college, which includes room and board, tuition and fees, money for books, and even an estimated amount for personal expenses and travel back and forth to the school.

The difference, if there is one, between the two numbers is how much need a family is eligible for.

Now, here's the exciting part.

The formula was written by crazy people. It makes no sense at all. If you own a business or are an entrepreneur, since I'm dealing with a government formula, you'll understand what I'm talking about. A lot of what they do doesn't make any sense.

But if you will take the time to understand what the rules are, you can legally and ethically lower your out-of-pocket cost by thousands or even tens of thousands of dollars a year.

For instance, having $10,000.00 in your student's name will raise what you are expected to pay by $3,500.00 . . . per year . . . or $14,000.00 over four years. In other words, you can actually lose more in aid than you saved by having the money in the wrong place! But, if you know the rules, it's usually pretty easy to move that money somewhere that it is exempt from being counted at all. And you just became eligible for a whole lot more money.

By the way, because most CPAs and financial planners are clueless to how this formula works (most don't even know it exists); their advice often is to put the money in the worst place possible. So, watch out around them!

Now, once you've gotten your EFC as low as legally possible, it's time to move on to step 2.

Step 2: You must research each school that your son or daughter is interested in for its financial aid history.

You've lowered your EFC, making you eligible for as much need as possible, but that doesn't mean anything—yet.

Next, we've got to research what each school historically offers to its students. I can't say that this information is readily available (I pay an absolute *fortune* to track these numbers in my office), but with a little digging, you should be able to find out a rough idea of what they offer.

Here are the three things you want to know for every school you're looking at.

What percentage of your need will they meet? Obviously, you want as close to 100% as possible, although with my clients, we're happy with anything over 80% of need met. In other words, if you have an EFC that has been reduced to $10,000.00, and your student is looking at a school that costs $35,000.00, you have a need at that school of $25,000.00. So, what we want to determine beforehand is how *much* of that $25,000.00 the school will help you with.

If the school will meet 80%, then you'll be getting $20,000.00 in financial aid, so you'll have to come up with your EFC of $10,000.00 plus the $5,000.00 the school will leave you short. So, in this case, you'll pay $15,000.00 out of pocket each year for a $35,000.00 school.

Next, you need to determine what percentage of the need that they meet is "gift" aid, or free money that *never* has to be paid back.

Let's stick with the example above for another moment. If the school was offering you 75% gift aid, that means that $15,000.00 of your $20,000.00 of aid would be free and $5,000.00 would be a "self help" program like work study or a low-interest loan.

This is critical to find out early because by knowing these numbers, you can determine what college will *really* cost you. Many times, you can have two schools that have the same cost of attendance, but one ends up being *much* cheaper because it meets a much higher percentage of need and gives away a lot more free money.

Step 3: Fill out all the financial aid forms accurately and on time.

Here is where most parents drop the ball.

First, many mistakenly assume that they don't qualify for any financial aid, and because the forms are a hassle (they *are* government forms after all), they don't even bother with them.

Huge mistake.

Always fill out whatever financial aid forms your colleges require—even if you think you make too much money.

The main form that the Department of Education uses is the FAFSA. It stands for Free Application for Federal Student Aid, and every school in the country uses it.

It's like filling out a tax return, and many of the questions are taken directly from your taxes.

However, here's something to watch for: According to the Department of Education, 92% of the FAFSAs are turned in with one or more errors on it, in many cases costing the parents a ton of financial aid. So, you want to plan ahead by knowing how to lower your EFC, but then you've got to make sure that your FAFSA is error free. The best advice I can give is to carefully read the directions and take your time with the forms.

Also, financial aid is given on a "first come-first served" basis, so you don't want to wait until the last second to turn in this and the other forms. In our office, we make sure to have all the financial aid paperwork completed for our clients no later than the end of January of the year the kid is going to school. So in other words, for the class of 2006, who will be leaving for college in the fall of 2006, we filled out the forms in January of 2006.

And because most people don't have their taxes for the previous year completed, it's perfectly acceptable to estimate your numbers. You just have to let the colleges know that's what you're doing.

In addition to the FAFSA, there is a whole host of other forms that schools require, and to get a financial aid award, you have to provide them with everything they ask for. It may seem frustrating and intrusive at times, but the payoff will be worth it. So, don't delay, and get them everything they ask for.

And, be proactive about checking with each school to make sure they've received what you sent them. You'd be surprised at how many times a student's award letter is delayed because the school has misplaced your documents. This can be a real problem if they've given away most of their money in the meantime, so stay on top of them.

Step 4: Don't be afraid to negotiate with the colleges.

The reason why you want to apply to six to eight schools is because you want to make sure that your student is accepted at more than one school so you have multiple offers on the table. Many schools will compete with other schools for students (even though they all deny the practice) or will give consideration to extenuating circumstances.

So don't be shy about politely explaining to a school that even though your child is thrilled to be accepted at their university, it will be much cheaper for them to attend another college that has offered a much better financial aid package. You'll be amazed at how often additional money will appear, just for the asking.

Also, you need to alert them to things that may not have shown up when you filled out your financial aid paperwork like a recent lost job, extensive medical bills, or things like that.

Step 5: Use tax-advantaged, low-interest ways to pay for college.

Even if you think you make too much money to get any aid, there are *always* ways to save thousands for college.

For instance, how you pay for your share, whether you pay as you go, take student loans, or use home equity can have a dramatic impact on how much college really costs. So, by paying attention to all the details of your financing, you can save a ton.

Also, most entrepreneurs qualify for things like "tax scholarships," which are specific ways of paying for college on a tax-advantaged basis, that saves them thousands of dollars legally on their taxes, whether they get any financial aid or not, as well as saving tens of thousands of dollars in interest and fees that the colleges would normally charge them. I don't have the space in this chapter to go into details about how to use this tool because everyone's situation is slightly different, but the important thing is to understand that it exists.

There you have it. The five steps to really getting money for college, no matter what your situation. It might seem a bit overwhelming at first, but by following my steps you will save yourself a mountain of cash, taxes, and interest on the college process.

No doubt, you can put that money to much better use.

Ron Caruthers is the nation's leading expert on money for college. He also assists his clients and their children with every aspect of college and career planning. Since 1995, he has assisted 1,125 families. He and his associates work with clients throughout the United States. For more information about Ron's services, the tax scholarship programs, and other money for college programs, visit www.collegeplanninginc.com or call (760) 438-9095. You can also sign up for free e-mail tips on college planning and funding at the web site.

Do You Make Mistakes with Your Credit?

Stephen Snyder

Fifteen years ago it didn't matter. You applied for as much credit as you wanted, and as long as you paid your bills on time, your credit rating was good. That's all changed. You are now scored. Lenders now use credit scoring to determine not only if they will offer you credit but also what interest rate they will offer you. So depending on that score, you may pay tens of thousands of dollars more or less on your home mortgage, thousands of dollars more or less on your auto purchase, or thousands of dollars more on business equipment purchases. Even insurance companies now use credit scores to determine who they will or won't insure and how much they'll charge. In fact, your credit score is now one of the most important numbers in your life.

Until recently, these credit scores and the means by which they are calculated was a closely guarded secret kept from consumers. Beginning in 2003, you were able to get access to your scores. Right now, you can get all three of your credit scores, a detailed report explaining your scores, and more helpful information at www.myfico.com/12. And this inquiry will NOT lower your credit scores, as many types of credit inquiries do.

Of course, knowing your scores is one thing, knowing what to do about managing and improving them is another. As an entrepreneur, busy and occupied with your regular business responsibilities, you may immediately think this too trivial to justify your time and attention. You'd be wrong. Actually, one of the easiest, quickest, and surest ways to improve your lifestyle is to deliberately improve your credit scores. You can live wealthier for less, by paying the lowest possible interest on everything. And if you happen to be a real estate investor, this takes on even greater importance and value.

I've identified 38 major mistakes most people unknowingly make that negatively affect their credit scores. Many seem like the right things to do, yet they actually lower your credit scores instead of improving them. Some of the most frequently made mistakes are:

- #3: Having unnecessary credit inquiries
- #4: Using lenders that do not report your credit accurately
- #6: Maxing out credit card limits
- #11: Closing credit accounts
- #16: Using cash
- #19: Transferring credit card balances to get a better interest rate

#22: Paying off installment credit accounts early

#25: Not increasing credit limits when you can

#29: Using personal credit for business—something entrepreneurs tend to be sloppy about!

Incidentally, even if you've gone bankrupt, you can recover quickly, and you can establish excellent credit scores quickly. One of the things I talk candidly about in my Home Study Program, "Increase Your Credit Scores—Improve Your Lifestyle," is my own recovery from bankruptcy years ago, and how I went from credit scores in the low 600s to over 800, and how I've achieved financial independence.

Like most people reading this book, I'm an entrepreneur, now with several large businesses, and an active real estate investor. I think the management of credit scores is one of the things most entrepreneurs overlook as a serious wealth strategy. Simply put, you can spend a lot less for the lifestyle you want by paying a little bit of attention to managing your credit scores, credit, and debt wisely—leaving more money available to invest, to build wealth.

Stephen Snyder has appeared on CNN, CNBC, Bloomberg TV, and been quoted in Parade Magazine, Newsweek, *and* The Wall Street Journal *as a respected expert on credit scores. He is the author of the book* Do You Make These 38 Mistakes With Your Credit? *For more information, visit www.increase yourcreditscores.com and www.38mistakes.com.*

Why Smart Entrepreneurs Need Smart Financial Advisors

Dennis Tubbergen

The world of money has gotten exponentially more complicated in recent years. There are now almost twice as
many mutual funds and other packaged investments
than there are stocks to put in them. Due to the fact that the U.S.
tax code is now over seven million words and growing every day
with a constant stream of IRS revenue rulings, revenue procedures and private letter rulings, it's extremely difficult for a busy
entrepreneur and his current advisors to stay on top of everything that's important in the financial arena. That task remains
challenging for me and my team of advisors, tax experts, attorneys, and other specialists, and it's our full-time endeavor. I

could go on giving you many more examples, but the point I want to make is that no entrepreneur should go very long or far without assembling a team of truly expert financial advisors and specialists who are looking out for his best interests.

I work with over 2,000 financial advisors, attorneys, CPAs, registered investment advisors, and insurance agents all across the country. I am president of an investment advisory company that directly manages over $50 million in client funds on a discretionary basis and tens of million more on a nondiscretionary basis. I am often called upon by financial advisors, attorneys, and accountants to develop customized tax reduction plans, estate plans, and business succession plans and to restructure existing portfolios for efficiency.

There are a lot of good reasons you need one—or more likely, several—of these experts working on your behalf:

1. As noted, there's way too much going on in the world of money, taxes, and investments for you to follow and be knowledgeable about.

2. It's likely that your regular CPA can't be relied on to bring you all the information that's necessary to accomplish all your financial goals. Why? Frankly, many CPAs aren't proactive when it comes to saving you money on taxes or seeking out new strategies to reduce taxes that come about when the IRS makes changes in the tax code. CPAs tend to record history, analyze what happened, and properly document these historical facts for the IRS. Some CPAs do offer sound financial advice, but many simply don't go far enough to help you preserve and create wealth, save taxes, and achieve maximum financial benefit from your business.

3. You may miss exciting financial opportunities. Many entrepreneurs are focused on and very good at making money, but they usually work harder than they need to for a lot longer than they'd have to in order to reach their financial goals and desired levels of wealth. They get so busy "making," they give little time or attention to "multiplying" through tax savings opportunities and other financial strategies. Many opportunities are overlooked.

4. You are unnecessarily vulnerable. Without expert advice, assistance, and even nagging, most entrepreneurs leave more of their wealth than necessary locked up inside their businesses rather than extracting it as they go through better investing, overlooked tax savings strategies, and unique wealth extraction methods. As the old axiom goes, too many eggs in one basket is just not a wise strategy.

5. Many entrepreneurs that I've ever worked with—including many with good CPAs—still overpay taxes. They pay far more than is legally necessary because they are too busy and running too fast to get creative, expert advice on a wide variety of different strategies for tax reduction. Sure, you've probably set up a retirement plan like a 401(k), Keogh, simple IRA, or SEP/IRA, but these strategies are really just deferral strategies. Although these strategies are appropriate for many entrepreneurs, there are other tax savings strategies that aren't deferral based, they're deduction based. The difference? Deferral simply means that you deduct something now and you must claim it as income later. Many deduction-based strategies don't have that kind of trade off; they simply offer immediate tax savings.

Frankly, dumb entrepreneurs operate all out of balance with too much time and energy given to making money and too little focus on wealth building. And as Dan Kennedy points out, income is perishable. Income is NOT an asset. You need to convert income into wealth deliberately and systematically. That's where the right team of knowledgeable advisors comes in.

We live in the age of ultraspecialization. If you need heart surgery, you don't rely on your family doctor. If you own an exotic sports car or luxury automobile, you don't take it to the mechanic at the corner garage. You shouldn't take your wealth development to any ordinary accountant or CPA either.

So, how do you find and choose an advisor or advisors to work with? It's not easy, but it is important. Every day that you procrastinate and put this off may add a hundred days to your work life. Costly mistakes may be made. Once made, money is lost forever to taxes that could be diverted to productive investments. I cannot urge you strongly enough to make the time right now, this week, to seek out and interview one or several advisors, and settle on one to get some "money diagnosis" and advice from.

To help, here are a few tips:

- Because many advisors out there are not really advisors at all but rather product salespeople, ask your prospective advisor to identify tax savings in your current financial situation. Ask him specifically how much the savings would be and ask him to explain how these savings will be obtained. Get some results BEFORE you hire him. Taxes are probably the most overlooked area and, ironically, often offer the greatest area of opportunity.

- Get referrals. If an advisor doesn't have a track record of getting results for busy, affluent entrepreneurs, you don't want him using you for a case study.
- Ask about his support team. At a minimum, in today's highly complex world of money and taxes, an advisor should be using three other professionals to help with your money diagnosis: a qualified asset protection specialist, a qualified tax planning specialist, and a qualified portfolio design specialist.

Why won't you follow this advice and seek out a top advisor to work with? There are four main reasons.

1. *Procrastination.* Putting it off until you have more money to invest or until some event or benchmark is reached. But then there's always another reason just around the corner, always another reason to wait. Tomorrow never comes.

2. *Being too busy.* The bottom line is that most entrepreneurs go their entire lives "too busy" making their livings and making their businesses work to actually extract, create, and multiply wealth. For as long as you are in business, you'll be working on and in your business. But you *can* put money to work for you and let it work to multiply itself without requiring your day-to-day attention or time. In many cases, a savvy advisor can find money you're now literally wasting, through overpaying taxes or letting it sleep idle, generating little or no yield. He can then make it work for you in vehicles that require little of your time.

3. *Being intimidated.* Many entrepreneurs feel that they can never understand all the ins and outs of investments, tax strategies, and wealth-building techniques, so it is easier

and more comfortable to avoid serious discussions. However, one of the marks of a top advisor is his ability to simplify the complex and present strategies to you that you can quickly and easily grasp and intelligently decide on.

Quite simply, these are not legitimate, good reasons to avoid dealing with personal wealth development. They are actually excuses for failure. After all, you do have a plan for your business. You need a wealth plan, too. And not one from some off-the-shelf software program, a fill-in-the-blank template plan. You need and deserve a customized plan prepared by a top advisor who takes the time to understand you, your business, your family, and your objectives.

To find information about different kinds of advisors and financial services professionals who follow my philosophies and strategies, you can go to www.taxsmartadvisor.com. (To subscribe to Mr. Tubbergen's weekly Financial Opportunity White Paper via e-mail, go to www.dennistubbergen.com.)

If you happen to be a financial advisor, financial planner or Registered Investment Advisor interested in strategies that can benefit your clients and/or in sources of good, new clients, you should get a free report from Mr. Tubbergen's office, "Cutting Edge Financial Strategies." Request it by fax at (800) 521-7856; ask for the report by name and include your name, address, and e-mail address with your request.

About the Author: Dennis Tubbergen, president of USA Wealth Management, is author of three monthly newsletters: for consumers, for financial advisors, and for financial professionals. He is a frequent speaker at industry events and has over 20 years of experience working in wealth development for his own clients and with over 2,000 financial advisors and tax professionals nationally. He is the creator and host of the Magic Money radio show and writes and produces two monthly audio productions: "Seminar on Tape" for consumers and a series for financial professionals. He has pioneered the team approach in tax and financial planning and is often hired by financial professionals to consult with them on complex planning cases.

There are many who find a good alibi far more
attractive than achievement.

—Eric Hoffer

Making money as an entrepreneur and making
excuses are mutually exclusive,
wholly incompatible.

—Dan Kennedy in *No B.S. Business Success*

The successful man or woman is the person who
can say, "This is the goal I am working toward.
And this is the way I'm going to get there. And
when I reach that goal, I'll have others by that
time, and I'll use this same system—improved
by then—to reach those goals as well."

—Carl Nightingale

WEALTH RESOURCES

Introduction to Wealth
Resources

*E*ntrepreneurs need a lot of two things: resourcefulness and resources.

Resourcefulness is the ability to take whatever resources you've got and can get and to turn them into what you want. To invent, innovate, and implement. To overcome obstacles and adversity. To get things done.

To some extent, you need resources to be resourceful. Even a Boy Scout needs two dry sticks and some how-to information in order to start a fire.

I have been an aggressive gatherer of information my entire life. Whenever confronted with a new opportunity or problem, my first response is to gather information, and my second to find experts. I want to know as much as I can before I act. That doesn't mean paralysis of analysis or endless procrastination. Fortunately, there is a wealth of information readily available about just about any subject, and I think it's tragic and mystifying that so many people—entrepreneurs included—choose bumbling and stumbling in the dark instead of the sure and steady progress more likely with the illumination of information.

I have also been an avid reader all my life. I read autobiographies and biographies of successful people for insight, ideas, inspiration, and encouragement. I read business books, self-improvement books, and how-to books in every area of interest. I am shocked when I encounter entrepreneurs who don't read!

In this section, I've provided my short list of mandatory reading on wealth. It is by no means an exhaustive or complete list, and for the sake of brevity, it omits many books, periodicals, and newsletters I regularly read or own and reread from time to time. I mean no disrespect to any author whose works I've omitted. I've tried to build more of a starter list here. Also in this section, I've listed people I think you need to "meet," if not in person, then through their web sites, newsletters, seminars, books, or other resources. Again, I've omitted many that would make a complete and exhaustive list with no disrespect or slight intended. Also, there's contact information for just about everybody mentioned in the book.

First, though, a few thoughts about resources from two of my speaking colleagues, men I respect, recommend, listen to, and have benefited from a great deal

Jim Rohn is one of the foremost success philosophers living today. I have been influenced by Jim's work from very early in my career, have been privileged to appear on programs with him, and have had him speak at one of my conferences. I frequently use Jim's statement: "Rich people have big libraries, poor people have big TVs. It is not coincidental." Here are a few more thoughts from Jim:

"The book you don't read won't help."

"Don't just read the easy stuff. You may be entertained by it, but you will never grow from it."

"Miss a meal if you have to, but don't miss a book."

"Everything you need for your better future has already been written. It's all available. All you have to do is go to the library. But only 3% of the people in America even have a library card. They're free."

"Would you like to guess how many people make wealth a study? Very few. Considering the many men and women who seek wealth and happiness, you'd think they would make a careful study of wealth. Why they don't is in that special category I call 'mysteries of life.'"

You can get more information about Jim Rohn's books, audio programs, and seminars at www.jimrohn.com, by calling (800) 929-0434, or by sending a fax to (972) 401-2003, and I urge doing so. Please mention that you read about Jim in this book when you call or write.

Brian Tracy is the most amazing compiler, organizer, and teacher of information I have ever known. He has written dozens and dozens of books, recorded hundreds of hours of programs, and always seems to be bringing more information forward. He's been at it for more than 25 years and speaks to more than 100,000 people a year—with Harvey Mackay *(Swim with the Sharks)*, Denis Waitley *(Psychology of Winning)*, and me! Brian and I have appeared together at over 100 events, and I've had Brian speak at my conferences as well. Significantly, Brian's own journey began as an itinerant laborer, devoid of direction in life, with no money and no apparent means of getting beyond a low-wage, low-income, low-lifestyle existence. He rose to success as an entrepreneur and to prominence as an advisor to CEOs of many of America's most prestigious corporations. Here's what Brian says about "feeding the mind":

> *Feed your mind constantly with words and images and input consistent with the direction in which you are growing. Read books and magazines for personal and professional development. Listen to educational audio programs at every opportunity. The more you read, listen, and learn about any subject, the more confident and capable you feel in that area. As you improve your inner understanding, you automatically improve your outer results.*

Brian also says this about "association":

> *Get around the right people. Because of the strong suggestive influence that other people have on you, for good or ill, you must be extremely careful about who you choose to spend your time with. Dr. David McClelland of Harvard found, after 25 years of research, that a choice of a "negative reference group" was in itself enough to condemn a person to underachievement or failure in life. Your reference groups are the people you associate with (as well as the books you read).*

To get more information about Brian's books, audio programs, and seminars, go to www/briantracy.com, call (619) 481-2977, or send a fax to (619) 481-2977. I urge you to do so. Please mention that you read about Brian in this book when you call or write.

In closing, I want to tell you one little "brag story" that makes a good point. Very early in his work as a speaker and author, Mark Victor Hansen made a list of all the people he wanted to meet personally. You may know Mark as co-author of the *Chicken Soup for the Soul* series or the book *One-Minute Millionaire*. Today, he is a multimillionaire entrepreneur involved in a dizzying array of business, charitable, and publishing endeavors. It wasn't always that way. Mark was once bankrupt and starting over, driving an old, battered car, struggling to get traction. That's when he made his list of people he admired, people who inspired him, people he viewed as influential who might assist him in achieving his goals, people he intended to meet. He has systematically met just about all of those on that list. I'm pleased to say my name was there.

The point is, he made a list. I, too, keep lists of people I intend to meet, the next books I will read, the information I need and am seeking. You should, too. Hopefully, the information on the following pages will help.

Books to Read/People to Meet for Wealth Development

Money/Wealth

The Millionaire Next Door by Thomas Stanley is the seminal research study, the inside peek at how millionaires, especially millionaire business owners, actually make, preserve, invest, and spend their money, think about money, and grow wealth. Your money education is incomplete without studying this book and Stanley's other works.

The One-Minute Millionaire by Mark Victor Hansen and Robert Allen. Robert Allen was a pioneer in the "no money down" real estate movement. Mark is one of the most visionary entrepreneurs I know. Together, they are best-selling authors and dynamic promoters. This book addresses thinking about wealth in an important way. Contact: www.markvictorhansen.com.

Think and Grow Rich, Laws of Success, Grow Rich with Peace of Mind, and *Master Key to Success* by Napoleon Hill, and *The Success System that Never Fails* by W. Clement Stone. These men defined the success philosophy that just about all subsequent authors, lecturers, and coaches in the field have studied. In one survey, more CEOs ranked *Think and Grow Rich* as the most influential book they'd ever read than any other except the *Bible.* Contact: www.napoleon hill.com, www.thinkandgrowrich.com.

The Virtue of Prosperity by Dinesh D'Souza. From the perspective of an immigrant, D'Souza explores the America dream, the virtues and responsibilities of prosperity, and a number of polit-ical/emotional issues about wealth. Again, I do not agree with everything in the book, but I recommend it because it is especially provocative.

The Trick to Money Is Having Some by Stuart Wilde. You really MUST get and read this book. If you are "pulling your punches," this may set you straight!

The Richest Man in Babylon by George S. Clason. A classic "fable" that presents the fundamentals of thrift and personal wealth.

Atlas Shrugged by Ayn Rand. This is, in my opinion, the most important novel ever written.

Business/Entrepreneurship

Sex, Money, KISS by Gene Simmons. Gene created the rock band KISS over 30 years ago. KISS continues as a juggernaut of licensing and merchandising, with over 2,000 licensed products, including KISS Kaskets, Kondoms, and VISA credit cards! Most people are unaware of what an extraordinary entrepreneur Gene is. In my opinion, this book is one of the most truthful business books ever written. Contact information: www.genesimmons.com.

Start with No by Jim Camp. Jim is a top negotiator and negotiation coach with a different take on the subject that I found refreshing, provocative, and useful. Contact: www.CampMethod.com.

Winning Through Intimidation, recently republished as *To Be Intimidated or Not to Be Intimidated*, and *Action!* by Robert Ringer. He's one of my favorite authors, and his original book has had as much or more influence on my business modus operandi than any other book. Contact information: robertjringer@hotmail.com, fax (703) 754-0955.

The Brand Called You by Peter Montoya. While I do not agree wholeheartedly with everything Peter advocates—and usually counsel that you should build brand as a by-product of direct-response advertising—my own wealth and that of many of my clients is absolutely, directly linked to powerful personal branding. Contact: www.petermontoya.com.

Mastering the Rockefeller Habits by Verne Harnish. A practical how-to book about growing, and increasing the value of a business. If you must have employees (which I no longer do), Chapter 2 is indispensable.

General Success

Success Is an Inside Job by Lee Milteer. Many of my clients put all their students, clients, and associates in her Millionaire Mindset

Tele-Coaching Program, rapidly becoming the largest of its kind. Lee did much of the research work and served as interviewer on the audio in my Renegade Millionaire System. She is a gifted and capable success, peak performance, and prosperity coach. Contact: www.leemilteer.com.

The New Psycho-Cybernetics by Dr. Maxwell Maltz (with Dan Kennedy). I owe an enormous debt to Dr. Maltz and his work, and am very pleased to have had the opportunity of updating it. You cannot out-earn or "out-wealth" your self-image, so this is of prime importance. Contact: www.psycho-cybernetics.com.

Other Works by Dan Kennedy

The No B.S. Series

   No B.S. Sales Success (Entrepreneur Press)

   No B.S. Business Success (Entrepreneur Press)

   No B.S. Time Management for Entrepreneurs (Entrepreneur Press)

   No B.S. Direct Marketing for NON-Direct Marketing Businesses (Entrepreneur Press)

Make Millions with Your Ideas (Plume)

The Ultimate Marketing Plan (Adams Media)

The Ultimate Sales Letter (Adams Media)

The New Psycho-Cybernetics with Dr. Maxwell Maltz (Pearson)

Zero Resistance Selling (Prentice-Hall/Pearson)

The Ultimate Success Secret (www.dankennedyproducts.com)

Why Do I Always Have to Sit Next to the Farting Cat? (petethe printer.com)

Complete Catalog of Audio Programs: www.nobsbooks.com

Web Sites of Special Interest

www.nobsbooks.com

Information about all books in the No B.S. series, free sample chapters, bonus gifts for each book, and free e-mail courses for the *No B.S. Wealth Attraction* and *No B.S. Direct Marketing for NON-Direct Marketing Businesses* books.

www.dankennedy.com

Information about Dan Kennedy professional services, newsletters, and audio products. Also, Glazer/Kennedy Inner Circle annual Marketing and Moneymaking SuperConference and annual Information Marketers' Summit.

www.renegademillionaire.com

Information about Dan's Renegade Millionaire System and annual Renegade Millionaire Retreat.

www.nationalsalesslettercontest.com

Information about the sales letter/marketing plan contest, featuring a new Ford Mustang as top prize. No purchase required to enter.

www.petetheprinter.com

Home of DONE4YOU publications and services, including ready-to-use customer newsletters for any business, featuring Dan Kennedy content. Also, two special Dan Kennedy publications: *No B.S. INFO-Marketing Letter* (only for information marketers) and *Look Over Dan's Shoulder* (for direct-response marketers and copywriters).

www.psycho-cybernetics.com

Dr. Maltz and Maltz/Kennedy publications.

www.entrepreneurpress.com

Official site of Entrepreneur Press.

www.northfieldpark.com

Dan's "home track," where he races his harness horses.

People Included in this Book

In this Resource Directory, you will first find people mentioned in the book whom you might want to contact, listed in order of first appearance, by page number. A much more extensive, frequently up-dated Resource Directory is provided to all Glazer-Kennedy Inner Circle Members who receive my *No B.S. Marketing Letter*, and you can arrange a free three-month membership with no obligation at www.dankennedy.com.

Dr. Paul Searby   Page 57
Fax: (281) 355-5449

Yanik Silver   Page 58
Fax: (301) 770-1096

Chet Rowland   Page 58
Fax: (813) 926-0657

Craig Proctor   Page 58
Fax: (905) 853-6078
Web site: www.craigproctor.com

Ron Romano   Page 58
Automated Marketing Solutions, Inc.
Fax: (800) 858-5753
Web site: www.findmeleads.com

Rob Minton   Page 58
Fax: (440) 918-0347

Matthew Gillogly   Page 59
Fax: (877) 202-8252

Dean Cipriano   Page 59
Fax: (856) 769-5055

Tracy Tolleson   Page 59
Tolleson Mortgage Publications Inc.
Fax: (602) 269-3113

Scott Tucker   Page 59
Fax: (773) 327-2842

Ron LeGrand   Page 60
Fax: (904) 260-8463
Web site: www.GlobalPublishingInc.com

Dr. Barry Lycka   Page 64
Fax: (780) 425-1217

Darin Garman   Page 65
Fax: (319) 861-5659

Bob Higgins   Page 65
Fax: (530) 244-9680

Daniel Frishberg   Page 65
Fax: (713) 621-5401
Web site: www.themoneyman.com

Dr. Charles Martin   Page 68
Fax: (804) 320-1014
Web site: www.affluentpracticesystems.com

Mark Ijlal   Page 69
Fax: (248) 671-0457

Bill Hammond   Page 69
Fax: (913) 498-0184

Jeff Paul   Page 80
Fax: (630) 778-0019
Web site: www.jeffpaul.com

Bill Glazer   Page 81
Fax: (410) 825-3301

Mike Vance   Page 83
Fax: (440) 243-8754

Steve Miller   Page 90
Fax: (206) 874-9666

Mitch Carson   Page 90
Fax: (818) 707-1777

Mark Victor Hanson   Page 100
Web site: www.markvictorhansen.com

Jack Canfield   Page 100
Web site: www.jackcanfield.com

Susan Berkeley   Page 104
Fax: (201) 541-4867

Matt Furey   Page 121
Fax: (813) 994-4947
Web sites: www.mattfurey.com and www.psycho-cybernetics.com

Rory Fatt   Page 139
Fax: (604) 940-6902

Pete Lillo   Page 161
Fax: (330) 922-9833
Web site: www.petetheprinter.com

Lee Milteer   Page 162
Web site: www.leemilteer.com

Somers White   Page 174
Fax: (602) 840-5970

Jim Rohn   Page 270
Web site: www.jimrohn.com

Brian Tracy   Page 271
Web site: www.briantracy.com

Guest Experts

Thad Winston   Page 177
For information about Thad's services, visit www.thadwinston.com.

Rob Minton   Page 183
Visit www.QuitWorkSomeDay.com/wealth to learn more about
the Income For Life System and programs. Or contact his office
at (440) 918-0047 or via fax at (440) 918-0347.

Darin Garman   Page 195
For more information about Darin Garman, investments, heartland of America properties, and private funds, visit www.com-
mercial-investments.com or call (800) 471-0856 and enter an
access code: #4002.

Jeff Kaller   Page 207
For more information, visit www.mrpreforeclosure.com or call
(800) 646-2574 to receive your free information package and a two-
hour DVD "How to Cash in on Short Sales with Half the Work."

Stephen Oliver   Page 215
To learn more about Mr. Oliver's services, visit www.MileHigh
Franchise.com or call (800) 795-2695.

Jerry A. Jones   Page 223
Mr. Jones' books, *Practice Building Success, Volumes I & II*, are
available direct from the publisher at (800) 311-1390. You can
reach Jerry via fax at (503) 371-1299.

Ted Thomas   Page 231
To receive a free information package about tax lien investing
and complete home study manuals and courses, tele-classes, and
even buying trips to auctions, fax a request to Ted Thomas at

(321) 449-9938 or call (321) 449-9940, and ask for the offer from the *No B.S. Wealth* book.

Scott Tucker   Page 237
Scott provides seminars, coaching, and consulting for other mortgage brokers in the United States and Canada. Scott may be reached via fax only at (773) 327-2842.

Ron Caruthers   Page 243
For more information about Ron's services, the Tax Scholarship Programs, and other money for college programs, visit www.col legeplanninginc.com or call (760) 438-9095. You can also sign up for free e-mail tips on college planning and funding at the web site.

Stephen Snyder   Page 253
For more information about Mr. Snyder's services and products, visit www.increaseyourcreditscores.com and www.38mistakes.com.

Dennis Tubbergen   Page 257
To subscribe to Mr. Tubbergen's weekly *Financial Opportunity White Paper* via e-mail, go to www.dennistubbergen.com. If you are a financial advisor, financial planner, or Registered Investment Advisor, the free report *Cutting Edge Financial Strategies*, is available. Request it by fax at (800) 521-7856, ask for the report by name, and include your name, address, and e-mail address with your request.

About the Author

D AN S. KENNEDY has enjoyed a long career as a prominent speaker, consultant, business coach, and author. He has delivered over 2,000 compensated speeches and seminars, including 9 years on a 25+ city seminar tour, appearing repeatedly with Zig Ziglar, Brian Tracy, Tom Hopkins, legendary entrepreneurs, Hollywood personalities, broadcasters Paul Harvey and Larry King, even 3 former U.S. presidents and General Colin Powell. People routinely pay $2,000.00 to $12,000.00 each to attend his seminars and travel from all over the world to do it. His annual Renegade Millionaire Retreat is directly related to the subjects in this book, and more information is at www.renegademillionaire.com.

Dan is an accomplished entrepreneur who has started, built, bought, and sold businesses, licensed his name and brand, developed two large publishing businesses, and has semiretired at age 50. He is also an active real estate investor and owner of more than a dozen harness racing horses, most of which race at Northfield Park, where he drives professionally. (The cable network TVG often broadcasts Northfield Park racing on Monday and Wednesday nights, or you can visit www.northfield park.com, if curious.)

He currently works with a limited Private Client Group and two coaching groups, which have a waiting list. He only occasionally accepts new consulting or direct-response copywriting clients, or speaking engagements. All such inquiries should be directed to Kennedy Inner Circle Inc., fax (602) 269-3113.

His popular *No B.S. Marketing Letter,* monthly audio and tele-seminar programs, and special events are all owned and managed by Glazer-Kennedy Inner Circle, and information can be found at its web site, www.dankennedy.com.

Information about his other books in this No B.S. series is at www.nobsbooks.com.

Index

Free Offers and Resources
from Dan Kennedy

Free Stuff Linked to this Book

Contest

**ENTER THE NATIONAL
SALES LETTER & MARKETING PLAN CONTEST**

Compete for a new FORD MUSTANG and other
exciting prizes!

Have your best sales letter/marketing plan evaluated
by a panel of expert judges.

No purchase required.

Contest is connected to two new 2006 books
by Dan Kennedy:
The Ultimate Sales Letter
and
The Ultimate Marketing Plan.

All rules, details, and free registration at:
www.NationalSalesLetterContest.com